AUTISM

A Parent's Guide

Need — 2 — Know

Hilary Hawkes

First published in Great Britain in 2009 by
Need2Know
Remus House
Coltsfoot Drive
Peterborough
PE2 9JX
Telephone 01733 898103
Fax 01733 313524
www.need2knowbooks.co.uk

Need2Know is an imprint of Forward Press Ltd.
www.forwardpress.co.uk

Contents

Introduction

Autism is a neurological developmental disorder or condition that impairs the way a person communicates and interacts with others and the world. It is a life long condition and its onset is generally recognised in very early childhood.

The autism spectrum is very wide and those with the disorder may, at one end, be very severely affected and in need of a great deal of support simply to engage in everyday living. Others may be less severely affected and are described as having high functioning autism (HFA) or another kind of autism called Asperger's syndrome (AS). While those with high functioning autism and Asperger's have similar difficulties, their disorder can be less severe. Many who have these conditions learn to compensate and find ways of leading productive and successful lives on some levels.

This book, however, is about coping with autism when it affects a child more severely and when that child is said to be around the middle or lower end of the autism spectrum. For more appropriate information and advice about very high functioning autism and Asperger's, see *Asperger's Syndrome – The Essential Guide* (Need2Know).

The term autism spectrum disorder or ASD refers to the way autism varies in severity, with those severely affected at one end of the spectrum and those only mildly affected right at the other end. Neuro-typical (NT) refers to someone who is not affected by autism and whose brain make-up is considered 'normal'.

According to the National Autistic Society, over 500,000 people are thought to be affected by autism in the UK. Parents who discover their child has autism have often gone through a long period of wondering why their child is not meeting normal developmental milestones or why he/she is so different from their brothers and sisters. Parents may find that, at first, experts do not appear to listen closely enough to their concerns, or that they are told their child will 'catch up'. Worst of all they may blame themselves for their child's difficulties

'The autism spectrum is very wide and those with the disorder may, at one end, be very severely affected and in need of a great deal of support simply to engage in everyday living.'

When a diagnosis is finally reached, the whole family needs the understanding, support and information that will enable them to find the best way to help their child. This book is for parents who are at this starting point of finding out what autism actually is and want the basic information to start looking for interventions and coping strategies. It aims to explain what autism is and to show some of the ways in which support and help can be found. It will answer many of the questions a parent might have at this stage, such as:

- Why has my child got autism?
- How will we cope and where will we get support?
- What is an autism-friendly environment?
- What will happen with schooling?
- What can I do to help my child reach his/her full potential?
- How do I deal with other people's reactions to my child's behaviour?
- What could the future hold for my child?
- What benefits and financial help are available?

'Perhaps the best thing is discovering that the many strategies and interventions which have helped many thousands of other children with autism become more independent could help their child too.'

Perhaps the hardest thing for parents is accepting that their child will not have the life they might have had without the condition. And perhaps the best thing is discovering that the many strategies and interventions which have helped many thousands of other children with autism become more independent could help their child too.

It is important to remember that every child is unique – a special individual with their own personality, aptitude and abilities. By accessing information and support for yourself and perhaps through the trial and error of finding what works best for your own child, you can help them become all they can be. This is all any parent can do, whether their child has autism or not. By reading this book you will be taking one more positive step towards helping your child (and yourself) to live effectively and realistically with autism.

Acknowledgements

Thank you to all the parents who responded to my questionnaires about bringing up their child with autism. At their request for confidentiality I have changed or omitted names when using their ideas, insights and quotes in this book. Thank you to the different experts and professionals who read sections or individual chapters. A special thank you to both Sheila Coates, retired head of service for Autism in Oxfordshire, who worked extensively with children and families affected by autism and who has co-authored books on autism, and Sarah Hendrickx (autism/Asperger's expert, trainer and author) for reading the whole manuscript and making useful comments and suggestions.

Disclaimer

This book is primarily a collection of research and the author advises that she does not claim medical qualifications. Anyone with concerns about their child's autism should consult their GP or healthcare professional for individual medical advice. This book is for general information about autism and is not intended to replace professional medical advice. Following programmes of therapy or taking medication should only ever be done under the advice and supervision of a medical, mental health or other appropriate professional.

Chapter One

What is Autism?

History

Before the 20th century there were few recordings of individuals who had autism-type behaviours. It wasn't really until the last century that doctors and researchers realised that there were children and adults with similar characteristics and difficulties.

In 1911, Eugen Bleuler, a Swiss psychiatrist, first used the term 'autistic'. However, he was referring to adults with a very different condition: a mental illness called schizophrenia.

In America, Leo Kanner wrote about the unusual characteristics some of the children in his clinic portrayed. He noted that their problems could include an inability to empathise with others, a need for sameness and routine, a fascination for objects and muteness or unusual speech. He published papers about his findings in the 1940s.

Around the same time, an Austrian physician, Hans Asperger, wrote about children in his clinic who displayed similar social disabilities to Kanner's patients but who were verbal and highly intelligent. This type of condition became known as Asperger's syndrome (AS).

It was realised that a wide spectrum existed, with Kanner's lower functioning patients at one end and Asperger's higher functioning patients at the other.

It wasn't really until the 1960s that professionals began to realise that a condition called autism was present in some children who displayed symptoms from a very early age, and that their condition was not due to upbringing or any other mental disorder.

'In 1911, Eugen Bleuler, a Swiss psychiatrist, first used the term "autistic".'

In the 1970s, psychiatrists Judith Gould and Lorna Wing concluded from their research that Kanner and Asperger had been talking about the same condition and that this condition existed on a continuum. The term 'autistic/autism spectrum' was coined and is still used to describe the different degrees of autism impairment. At the more severe end, the condition became known as severe/classic autism or Kanner's syndrome. At the higher functioning end, the autism became known as high functioning autism (HFA) and Asperger's syndrome. Between the two extremes are conditions often called pervasive developmental disorder not otherwise specified or PDD-NOS.

Severe/classic or Kanner's autism/syndrome

These children are the most severely affected. They are very often non-verbal and can have very extreme sensory intolerances.

Pervasive developmental disorder not otherwise specified

Children with PDD-NOS are developmentally delayed with symptoms of autism. Originally, Asperger's syndrome was included in this group.

Rett syndrome and fragile X

These two conditions are not autism but those affected have autism-type characteristics and difficulties. Rett syndrome mainly affects girls. A child with Rett syndrome develops normally at first, then Rett develops when something goes wrong with the genetic make-up of the developing baby, but it is not hereditary. People with Rett syndrome usually have profound multiple learning disabilities.

Fragile X syndrome is an inherited mental impairment disorder caused by a fragile X chromosome (one of the chromosomes which helps determine the sex of a baby). Those affected can have language, behavioural, social and

'It wasn't really until the 1960s that professionals began to realise that a condition called autism was present in some children who displayed symptoms from a very early age, and that their condition was not due to upbringing or any other mental disorder.'

emotional difficulties. They may also have distinct physical features such as large, long faces, overcrowded teeth, flat feet or double jointedness. It is the most common known cause of inherited mental disability.

Asperger's syndrome and high functioning autism

Children with Asperger's syndrome and high functioning autism have normal to well above average intelligence, but impairment of social imagination, communication and interaction. While they may eventually lead normal and fulfilling lives, they may suffer high anxiety levels and need routines and sameness. Because they are aware that they are 'different' from their neuro-typical peers, they may be prone to feelings of low self-worth, loneliness or depression. They also suffer from sensory intolerances.

There is some debate amongst professionals as to the difference between Asperger's syndrome and high functioning autism. The two conditions have their own diagnostic criteria, and some experts say that the differences can include someone with Asperger's syndrome having some motor or movement impairment in addition to social interaction, imagination and communication problems and someone with high functioning autism having fewer language skills.

Signs and characteristics of autism

Early signs

If your child has been diagnosed with autism or you suspect he or she may have the condition, you may have noticed some of the following features from early babyhood:

- A feeling that something was not right from the start.

- Normal development in the early months, or for the first year or two, and then a sudden change or regression.

- Either your child being unusually placid and undemanding or extremely fretful and difficult to settle.

- 'Floppiness' – when picked up your child did/does not reach to hold you.

- Feeding problems – an inability to suck well.

- Fascination for visual stimuli such as repetitively moving objects or lights, but little or no interest or reaction to people's faces.

- Lack of eye contact.

- Late sitting, crawling or walking.

- No crawling stage.

- No speech or unusual speech development.

- Failure to attract your attention to something that interested them by pointing or verbal exclamation.

Experts believe that a combination of some of these features can indicate that a young child is affected by autism. The features can mean that the child is self-absorbed and not naturally interested in people or the world around them.

However, it is important to remember that other influences or illness can cause a baby or young child to temporarily lose interest in things going on around them too – talk to your GP for advice.

'Diagnosticians look for a "triad of impairment" in order to formally diagnose autism.'

Later features

Diagnosticians (in this case, experts at diagnosing autism) look for a 'triad of impairment', or three areas of impairment, in order to formally diagnose autism. This range of disability was first mentioned by autism expert and psychiatrist Lorna Wing. The three areas of impairment referred to are:

- Impairment of social interaction.

- Impairment of social communication.

- Impairment of social imagination.

Social interaction impairment

Lorna Wing, author of *The Autistic Spectrum*, divides children with autism into four groups when describing the different types of social interaction impairment:

- The aloof group – these children can show no interest in the emotions or feelings of others even if another person is distressed or in pain. They may use others to get what they want if they cannot get it themselves and then return to ignoring these people again. They may make little or no eye contact and do not respond when spoken to or called.

- The passive group – children in this group seem more able to play with other children. They are compliant and amenable and other children like to include them in their games. However, they may not initiate social contact themselves.

- The 'active, but odd' group – these children may initiate social contact but do so in inappropriate ways. They may stare when attempting to make eye contact, hug people who don't want to be hugged, ignore the needs of other children around them and can become aggressive if their needs are not met.

- The over formal, stilted group – here the child may appear over polite and formal towards others. They appear to be following rules of social interaction but do so without really understanding.

Social communication impairment

Some children with autism are non-verbal and a small minority remain non-verbal as they get older. The majority do speak but have a variety of difficulties when doing so. Parents may notice any of the following:

- Confusing one word with another

- Difficulties with personal pronouns (I, he, we, she). The child may refer to him/herself in the third person, i.e. 'He/she is hungry' instead of 'I am hungry'.

- Non-conversational type speech, i.e. the child talks at great length but disregards the input of others.
- A tendency to talk about the same things without realising others do not want to hear it again.
- Unusual vocal prosody, i.e. lack of variety in tone, pitch, etc.
- A lack of understanding of non-verbal communication, e.g. nodding or shaking the head, and a lack of understanding of facial expression.
- Echoing others' speech (called 'echolalia'). This is where the child repeats back the words someone else has just said instead of responding in a conversational way.

Social imagination impairment

Children with autism also have difficulties with social imagination. This means that they find it difficult to work out what people are thinking or how they are feeling. They may not be able to predict the consequences of their actions, including realising when they may be in danger. Having poor social imagination also means the child will find coping with change stressful. The child may not be able to play imaginative games.

Other characteristics

Ways to deal with these difficulties are discussed further in chapter 4. Other characteristics you may have noticed as a parent include the following.

Repetitive behaviour

Your child might shake or flap their hands or arms, rock their whole body backwards and forwards or bang their head against the floor or wall.

'Children with autism also have difficulties with social imagination. This means that they find it difficult to work out what people are thinking or how they are feeling.'

Repetitive routines

You may have noticed that your child has particular rigid routines – he/she may insist that things are always done in exactly the same way. If you try to change this, the variation might cause your child such extreme stress that the whole task or activity has to be started all over again. Some routines may be in connection with everyday tasks such as putting on shoes or brushing teeth, or they may be routines made up by your child such as always wanting toys placed in a certain place or order around the room.

Motor or movement abnormalities

Your child may have fine or gross motor control problems. He/she may find tasks that require fine movement, e.g. tying laces or fitting lids on jars, very frustrating. Some children with autism have an odd gait or way of walking. This might be toe-walking, i.e. putting the toe and ball of the foot down before the heel, or walking without movement of the arms.

Sensory sensitivities

Being over or under sensitive to certain stimuli is a source of great anguish and frustration for a lot of children. Their heightened or underdeveloped senses are often the cause of many of their fears, intolerances and avoidance behaviours. An over sensitivity to some fabrics may mean the child can only wear certain types of clothes. Light and sound sensitivities may mean the child cannot cope in noisy environments such as large shops, crowds, playgroups or playgrounds and may react to such a stressful environment by screaming, running away or putting their hands over their ears.

Learning difficulties

Learning can be difficult for any child with autism – even high functioning and highly intelligent children. While being of high intelligence helps, there may still be problems with memory, processing information or working at class or

'Even those with autism who have a high IQ may find learning difficult due to memory, processing, imagination difficulties and team work requirements'

Sarah Hendrickx.

group pace. Some may have a visual rather than verbal style of learning. Some children on the autism spectrum may also be diagnosed as having dyslexia or another specific learning difficulty.

Digestive and eating problems

Research has found a connection between the functioning of the digestive system and autism. Many children with autism have a very restrictive diet which may be due to food intolerances or a dislike of trying anything new and unfamiliar.

Toilet training problems

It can be very difficult to toilet train a child affected by autism. If your child is beyond what is considered the usual age for obtaining bladder or bowel control, there may be a specific reason for this. Your child may not have the motivation or desire to gain control and be independent in this way. They may have grown used to the fact that you take charge of this. The usual methods for dealing with late toilet training may not work with a child who has autism – some are afraid of potties or the sight or sound of flushing toilets.

Epilepsy

Some children are also identified as having epilepsy, and the onset of seizures in adolescents is also common. You should see your GP or child's health professional in the first instance for more information on epilepsy. *Epilepsy – The Essential Guide* (Need2Know) is also an informative quick-read.

Sleep problems

Sleep problems may be due to the overactive mind of a child with autism, sensory sensitivities or anxiety, fears or discomfort. If your child has sleep problems and is unable to communicate with you, it can be very difficult to know where to begin in resolving the problem.

Special interests

Many children on the autism spectrum develop special interests. This is especially true of children with high functioning autism and Asperger's syndrome, where it can be considered a feature of those conditions. You may have noticed that certain activities, objects, tasks or toys keep your child absorbed and engaged to the point of obsessiveness. The special interest is likely to be a solitary and passive activity. Sometimes special interests evolve over time or suddenly develop into something entirely new.

Co-morbid conditions

A co-morbid condition is one that exists alongside the main disability or disorder. They can include:

- Obsessive compulsive disorder or OCD (an anxiety disorder and not the same as performing things in rigid routine manners).

- Tourette's syndrome (the repetitive performing of vocal or visual 'tics').

- Dyspraxia (a movement and co-ordination disorder).

- Dyslexia and attention deficit hyperactivity disorder (ADHD).

The majority of people with an autism spectrum disorder (ASD) have another co-morbid condition such as one of the above.

'Many children on the autism spectrum develop special interests. This is especially true of children with high functioning autism and Asperger's syndrome, where it can be considered a feature of those conditions.'

Summing Up

While every child with autism will be different, particular characteristics have been found in children diagnosed with the condition. Even though many of the usual parenting strategies that deal with some of these difficulties will not work with a child with autism, there is a great deal that can be done to support you, your child and your family. Further chapters of this book suggest interventions and strategies that parents and professionals have found useful and beneficial.

For further details of the features of autism, the National Autistic Society's (NAS) website provides an invaluable amount of information and links to other sources (see help list).

'Even though many of the usual parenting strategies that deal with some of these difficulties will not work with a child with autism, there is a great deal that can be done to support you, your child and your family.'

Chapter Two

Research into Autism

Do we know what causes autism?

The National Autistic Society describes autism as a development disorder which affects the way the brain processes information (www.autism.org.uk, Position statement: causes of autism).

Research shows that genetic and environmental factors trigger the condition. No single gene has been found to be responsible for the onset of the condition, but it is thought that several genes play a part in its presence. No evidence has been found to suggest parenting styles cause autism.

Types of research

Different types of research into the possible causes of ASDs and strategies that can alleviate some difficulties is always being carried out. Some of these research methods include gene testing and experimentation, brain scanning, biomedical interventions and behavioural interventions.

Genetic theories

Genetic research into the causes of autism is taking place in many parts of the world. Researchers are attempting to find the genes that are responsible for the onset of the condition. This is partly with the view to looking at whether, in the future, it will be possible to predict if a couple's children may have the condition and if genetic engineering to avoid spectrum disorders is a possibility. The ethical debate about whether we would want to limit or eliminate autism altogether is an important one. Many parents (and many

'Autism is not caused by a person's upbringing or their social circumstances and is not the fault of the individual with the condition.'

National Autistic Society, Appendix Three: Key Information About Autism.

people with autism themselves) would not want the condition to be totally eliminated and, while valuing all life, would wonder what the impact would be on science and society without the talents of some of those at the high end of the autism spectrum.

Within the same research area, some scientists and doctors are hoping to find ways of 'switching on' the genes that are believed to be 'switched off' in a person with autism.

The Autism Research Centre (ARC) in Cambridge is a good source of further information on this type of research and its consequences (see help list for the ARC's contact details). Cambridge researcher Professor Simon Baron-Cohen is one of the leading experts in the field and has written extensively around this interesting and much debated area.

'Researchers are attempting to find the genes that are responsible for the onset of the condition.'

Behavioural interventions

Many types of behavioural or social teaching interventions exist and are continually being developed. Their purpose is to help children and adults with ASDs to develop techniques that will enable them to cope with different situations and reach their full potential in life. This may be by the teaching of social skills, communication methods and means of recognising and controlling emotions. Many of these programmes are said to have been tried and tested by countless numbers of parents and professionals over past decades and include the Son-Rise programmes, applied behavioural analysis and TEACCH (Treatment and Education of Autistic and related Communication-handicapped CHildren) to name just a few. These and many other strategies are considered in more detail in chapter 4.

Biomedical theories

Biomedical theories suggest that the causes of autism lie in environmental factors which impact on the body and the immune system. They propose that the elimination or avoidance of these undesirable factors can improve the person's condition. Some researchers believe that allergies (including some food intolerances) are partly responsible for autism. These researchers believe that people with autism lack a special enzyme needed for the digestion and processing of certain proteins. This is the brain-gut connection debate.

There are also auto-immune or virus-induced theories of causation as well as the heavy metal poisoning theory. Virus-induced theories say that people with autism have immune system abnormalities which may have been partly damaged during pregnancy or very early development. The heavy metal poison theorists say that we are damaged by the interaction of metal in the environment – e.g. power plant emissions or lead based paint. Their theory suggests that the bodies of people with autism are unable to naturally excrete these damaging products and so a dangerous build-up ensues. See the Autism Medical or Autism Research websites for further details (see help list).

The MMR (measles, mumps and rubella) vaccination controversy emerged when the numbers of children aged between 18 and 24 months being diagnosed with autism increased. Some continue the debate about the effect of thimerosal (also known as thiomersal, a mercury that has been used as a preservative in vaccines) while others believe the link has been disproved. One place to read about the debate is the National Autistic Society website.

Brain scanning

Abnormalities in the neurotransmitter systems of the brain (the chemical messages of the brain) have been found in people who have autism.

Variations in the actual sizes of brains in people with autism have also been found. For example, areas of the brain that deal with orientation or perception of stimuli are differently sized in a brain not affected by autism. The overall brain size is also larger in children with autism.

The development of brain scanning images enables researchers to test which parts of the brain do what, in what way and how they differ from one another. Researchers can then compare the responses of patients with autism with non-ASD patients.

The MEG scanner (one of which is based at Oxford) enables doctors and researchers to investigate brain patterns with the aim of understanding the differences and developing strategies that may enable individuals with autism to compensate for some of their difficulties.

Research into cortisol levels

'The MEG scanner enables doctors and researchers to investigate brain patterns with the aim of understanding the differences and developing strategies that may enable individuals with autism to compensate for some of their difficulties.'

Cortisol is a stress hormone. We need it to react quickly and normally to changes that occur in our daily lives. We get a sudden release of cortisol shortly after waking and levels drop gradually during the rest of the day. Researchers at the Albert Einstein College and the University of Bath have found that children with autism do not have this normal rush of cortisol after waking but their levels do decrease as the day goes on. Researchers suggest that this may explain why children with autism or Asperger's syndrome dislike change and prefer sameness and routine. Without the correct level of cortisol, change causes them great stress and anxiety. Medication to keep cortisol at more normal levels may help children with autism experience less anxiety during changes to their routine.

For more information see 'New theories of autism, Asperger syndrome' by J M Grohol, which can be found at www.psychcentral.com, search for 'autism and cortisol'. This article is about research into cortisol levels in the brains of children with autism and Asperger's syndrome.

Summing Up

No parent of a child with a severely limiting condition wants to see their child struggle with the effects that such disorders can bring. Many who say that the talents of individuals with autism outweigh the difficulties they experience do so in the hope that the affected individuals are actually able to recognise and make use of their special abilities. Even more, they may say this in the hope that society makes allowances and special considerations so that those affected by autism are able to lead as full lives as possible. Sadly, this is not always the case.

Research into the causes and consequences of autism may, in time, suggest ways that the condition can be avoided entirely in the future. Parents, professionals and those with autism themselves may decide that this would be an unnecessary step in the wrong direction. More realistic is the hope that research will continue to discover and suggest interventions, medical and behavioural, that will enable children and adults affected by autism to lead happy, fulfilling and healthy lives – regardless of the good and bad effects of their spectrum disorder.

Chapter Three

Getting a Diagnosis

How do I get a diagnosis for my child?

A usual starting point is to talk to your GP. You might find it helpful to write down exactly what your concerns are, with examples of your child's behaviour. Jot down any thoughts other people have expressed too and tell your GP what you would like to happen, i.e. you would like your child referred for a specialist assessment.

What could my GP/health professional do?

Your GP will probably ask questions related to the development of your child, so the information in your child's red personal child health care booklet (currently used throughout the UK) may be useful. They also might make use of an initial assessment known as CHAT. CHAT stands for the Checklist for Autism in Toddlers and was developed by a team of researchers to help spot the signs of delayed development in social or communication skills. It is administered by a health visitor or GP at the child's 18 month check-up. You can view the questions asked on the CHAT website and also contact the organisation for further information if you wish (see help list). CHAT guidelines advise GPs and health visitors to repeat the test about a month later if a child does not score highly. If a child fails to score sufficiently again, they can be referred to a specialist for assessment. Children too old for the initial CHAT test need to be referred straight on to a specialist for diagnosis.

'Tell your GP what you would like to happen, i.e. you would like your child referred for a specialist assessment.'

In the event of your GP refusing to refer your child, you can contact the National Autistic Society for advice and lists of diagnosticians. The National Autistic Society also has its own diagnostic centre in London: the Lorna Wing Centre (see help list for National Autistic Society details).

How do I prepare my child?

If your child is older and able to understand that they are being taken along to a professional to be assessed, it is a good idea to give some sort of simple but truthful explanation. You will not want to cause your child anxiety, but some children feel even worse if they are worried about what will happen. If your child is unfamiliar with doctors, you should explain who they are and what they do. If your child is aware that they have particular problems, e.g. with obsessions, fears or an inability to cope socially or communicate, then you could mention that some doctors have a good idea about how to help them or how to find other special people who can.

'The diagnostician will ask questions related to social and emotional abilities and responses, communication, cognitive (learning) and movement skills.'

What happens during the diagnosis?

If your child is referred to a specialist so that they can be assessed for any possible communication/social disorders, you may have a long wait for the appointment. The alternative is to take the private route and some parents, especially those with older children, prefer to do that. Otherwise, it is just a question of waiting.

Diagnosticians in the UK may use one of two diagnostic criteria set out in the following official manuals:

- *The International Classification of Diseases*, (ICD-10),10th edition (World Health Organisation, 1992).

- *The Diagnostic and Statistical Manual of Mental Disorders*, (DSM-1V), 4th edition (American Psychiatric Association, 1994).

These consist of questions about different areas of development, ability and skills. The diagnostician will ask questions related to social and emotional abilities and responses, communication, cognitive (learning) and movement skills.

If you have a partner, it is helpful for you both to attend. The professional will want to ask a great variety of questions about your child's early development, behaviour and social and communication skills. Your answers will give the practitioner as full a picture as possible of your child's ability to interact, respond and think imaginatively. Remember, they are looking for the triad of impairment – impairment in social interaction, social communication and social imagination. This questionnaire with parents may be referred to as the ADI (Autism Diagnostic Interview).

If your child is very young, they will then be observed (possibly on more than one occasion) playing and interacting with a trained professional. With a slightly older child, the diagnostician will spend a session talking and playing with your child. They will engineer games and opportunities for social interaction and observe and assess how your child handles this. Such an assessment may be referred to as the ADOS (Autism Diagnostic Observation Schedule).

How do I cope with a positive diagnosis?

You may be told very quickly if autism is suspected or diagnosed. Your main questions may be similar to the following:

- What help can we get?
- How will we cope?
- What will the effect on the rest of our family be?
- What will our child's future be like?

Discovering that your child has a definite diagnosis of autism can be shocking, even if you half suspected that this would be the outcome. Some parents feel, incorrectly, that they are to blame for their child's autism. Other reactions may include grief, fear, anger or even disbelief. Getting as informed as possible about autism – from its causes to the many tried and tested interventions and strategies for helping your child and yourself – is part of the way that you can come to terms with the diagnosis.

You will almost certainly need to find someone to talk to. This might be a close friend or family member, a health professional involved with your family or a counsellor. Initially, you might like to consider:

- Contacting the National Autistic Society for information about their Help and Help2 programmes for parents of recently diagnosed children (see help list).

- Finding out if there are local support and information groups/organisations for other families of children with autism. See chapter 9 on getting support.

- Asking your GP for contact details of counsellors who have experience in helping families deal with diagnosis.

- Contacting Face2Face – an organisation that offers regular and ongoing support to parents by other parents who have a child diagnosed with a disability (see help list).

Who do I tell?

'Some parents decide there is no reason to hide the fact that their child has autism and will be prepared to tell anyone and everyone who comes into contact with them. Others prefer to disclose on a "need to know" basis.'

Some parents decide there is no reason to hide the fact that their child has autism and will be prepared to tell anyone and everyone who comes into contact with them. Others prefer to disclose on a 'need to know' basis. Those who need to know will include anyone who cares for your child or has contact with them through toddler/pre-school or school settings. You may find that mentioning autism explains any difficult behaviour your child may exhibit. If you fear that people will not understand or will react in discriminatory ways, you have the opportunity to explain what autism is and educate others into a fuller understanding.

There are a number of useful books and booklets available from autism resources – see the National Autistic Society website or ask your child's diagnostician. Some of these are brief but accurate and can be useful to give to other family members and will provide you with back-up as you try to explain. See the book list at the back for some ideas.

What will the diagnosis mean for my child?

A diagnosis of autism for your child means that the future will be different. This does not mean your child cannot have a happy childhood and adulthood. It does not mean they will not have interests and abilities that give them a lot of joy and sense of fulfilment. It does not mean your child will not have friendships and companionships. It does mean, however, that your child will approach and acquire all of these things in a different way. There will be some things your child will be unable to achieve, but with help, support and the right information, you can discover and develop your child's strengths.

What will the diagnosis mean for my family?

You will need to find some way of accepting and coming to terms with the diagnosis. This can be very difficult for many parents and can take time. Many parents describe going through a process of grieving for the child they thought they had but now know they do not have, then reaching a point where they realise the love they have for their child has not and will not change. They realise that their child has a special and unique personality and they are not defined by having autism. Understanding that there are many ways of helping your child achieve their full potential can give you goals to work towards and hope that many things can improve. None of us know what the future holds for our children whether they are affected by autism or not.

Your child's autism will alter the way you do things as a family and even what you do personally. Children with autism can demand a lot of attention and you will need to arm yourself with as much knowledge and support for yourself as you can.

Some parents say that post diagnosis, or at any point, counselling helps. Having a child with autism places a great strain on parents and many find their marriages suffer. You may feel that your entire life revolves around coping with your child. Counselling with someone knowledgeable and experienced in working with families affected by autism can be enormously helpful. For more details on how to find suitable support and counselling, see chapter 9.

'There will be some things your child will be unable to achieve, but with help, support and the right information, you can discover and develop your child's strengths.'

Effects on your other neuro-typical children

There is a great deal of research that suggests that the siblings of a child with a disability (including those with autism) can be profoundly affected. This may sound very obvious but often the effects can be unseen. Of course, there can also be many positive aspects to learning to accept and understand those with disabilities or difficulties at such a young age. The UK charity Sibs supports and advises child and adult siblings of people with disabilities. Sibs acknowledges that siblings may often feel isolated or that they do not get enough of their parents' attention. They may dislike the stares their brother or sister may attract from strangers in public and be alarmed by their sibling's difficult or unusual behaviour.

You can help your other children by:

- Teaching them as much as they can understand about autism.

- Emphasising their sibling's good points and the good times they have had together.

- Giving your neuro-typical children plenty of opportunities to have your full attention – including outings when their sibling is elsewhere.

- Encouraging their own interests and friendships and showing lots of interest and enthusiasm about these.

- Talking to your child about their concerns and encouraging them to do the same. Your child may have fears about whether their own children will have autism or whether they will have to look after their disabled sibling one day.

- Not expecting your neuro-typical children to act as babysitter to their sibling and not allowing them to be or feel responsible for their sibling.

- Getting information from Sibs (www.sibs.org).

If your neuro-typical children suffer emotionally, do not ignore this. Think about whether specialist counselling could support and help them – see chapter 9.

Summing Up

Discovering that your child has autism can be a shock to both you and your whole family. However, knowing for sure means that you can access support, advice and interventions that will benefit your child and help you as you find ways of enabling them to become as independent as they possibly can.

▪ Read and research as much as you can about autism.

▪ Use the National Autistic Society website for up-to-date information, news and advice.

▪ Get support for yourself and other family members when you need it.

▪ Don't allow yourself to feel isolated or alone – ask the professionals dealing with your child about any local support groups or places where you might meet other parents dealing with the same issues.

'Get support for yourself and other family members when you need it.'

Chapter Four

Living with a Child with Autism

Safety – an autism friendly home

One of the first things you can do as the parent or carer of a child with autism is to ensure that the child's home is as autism friendly as possible. This means organising and arranging an environment around the child that takes account of their sensitivities and intolerances. This does not mean giving your child everything they demand but more limiting or getting rid of anything that causes pain or too much distress. You should also emphasise anything that encourages your child to engage with the world or other people.

Children (and adults) with autism can have extreme sensitivity of any of the five senses: hearing, touch, sight, smell and taste. This is more than mere fussiness. Extreme sensory sensitivity can be the cause of many of the behaviour difficulties your child may demonstrate. One example is an inability to tolerate background noise – the child may find this painful and get very distressed or anxious.

Another problem is hyposensitivity – this is where the child appears to have an inability to experience or 'feel' a certain stimuli. One of the most worrying issues for parents is a child's inability to feel and react normally to pain. This can lead a child into potentially dangerous situations where they may simply carry on with what they are doing after injuring themselves.

As a parent you will already be familiar with the need to make a home 'toddler proof'. Making a home 'autism friendly' uses many of these common sense safety ideas alongside other practical modifications. Some of these ideas suggested by parents of children with autism are listed overleaf. You may find that some of the ideas will be unnecessary for your particular child; all children are different.

'Children (and adults) with autism can have extreme sensitivity of any of the five senses: hearing, touch, sight, smell and taste. This is more than mere fussiness.'

Indoors

- Put locks on cupboards that contain items you do not wish your child to damage.

- Put dangerous substances, e.g. cleaning liquids or sharp knives and scissors, either in locked cupboards or out of reach.

- Remember to keep keys where you can find them but where your child will not!

- Continue to use child-safety locks on other cupboards and electrical socket covers.

- Use radiator covers and fixed fire guards.

- If your child pulls on curtains, use Velcro fastenings instead of curtain rings as they can be easily re-hung.

- Patterned rugs or carpets can cause confusion for a child with autism when they try to walk across them. Plain soft furnishings and soft, light coloured décor is preferable.

- Put safety plastic over glass doors or glass table tops, or get rid of them.

- In large rooms or echoey hallways, use carpets and enough soft furnishings to absorb sound. Wooden or laminate floors reduce the absorption of sound in the home.

- It is worth investing in strongly-made furniture in all areas of the home.

- Consider fixing furniture to the floor in your child's bedroom.

- Use safety rails on upstairs windows.

- You may need to avoid using air fresheners if your child over-reacts to the strong odour, or find one your child can tolerate.

- Arrange furniture around the sides of the room so there are fewer objects to navigate.

- If possible, purchase your child's bedding and mattress from a company that manufactures extra strong, washable products.

- Check out the charity Fledglings which gives information and sells specialist equipment for children with a range of problems, e.g. incontinence padding for beds.

- It may be wise to keep hot water temperatures at a non-burning temperature.

- It is possible to purchase locks for toilet seats if your child has a fascination for putting things in the toilet.

- If your child picks pieces off plants to eat, be sure to keep them out of reach or consider getting rid of them altogether.

See the help list for contact details of useful resource and equipment suppliers.

Outside

- Make sure your garden is secure so that your child cannot wander off.

- Keep garden equipment and tools locked away.

- Avoid prickly or poisonous plants.

- Use safety glass in greenhouses.

- Some children with autism like the sound of glass breaking, so you might need to get rid of small objects and larger stones, pebbles, etc.

- Have some fun, robust and safe play equipment in the garden as this is a good place for your child to unwind and release energy. See the help list for details of some of the companies that make play equipment recommended for special needs children. For example, Fledglings can give advice on suppliers of hammocks and swings.

'Arrange furniture around the sides of the room so there are fewer objects to navigate.'

Getting out and about

You may find that actually managing to get out of the house with your child is an achievement in itself. The difficulties that you face en route and on arrival at your destination may present challenges. If your child has a diagnosis of autism, you are entitled to apply for a Blue Badge that will enable you to use disabled parking spaces (see chapter 8). These should mean that you can get a little closer to your destination and you may also have a wider parking space – useful for the often time-consuming job of fitting your child back into a safety seat.

You may find the following points useful:

- Investigate purchasing a large child pushchair (rather than a toddler or under-five's pushchair).

- If your child running away is an issue, consider purchasing an alert alarm that will let you know if your child is going astray. An identity bracelet may also be a good idea if you can get your child to wear it.

- Consider giving your child a tracking device, child safety tag or child wander alarm.

- Some parents dress their children in autism t-shirts/sweat shirts. These convey, in three or four words, that the wearer has autism and can be useful in alerting the general public who do like to stare at children (especially older ones) who are behaving in ways they may consider to be different to the norm. Badges saying that the wearer has autism are also available. One place to buy these is the National Autistic Society. See their online catalogue at www.autism.org.uk.

- A child harness (body or wrist fixing) may be useful for a younger or smaller child.

- The DVLA (Driver and Vehicle Licensing Agency) has details about special safety harnesses and car seats for older children with special needs. See the help list for contact details.

- Get a RADAR key so that your child can use the usually locked disabled toilets when out. This can avoid having to use larger facilities and negotiating queues and other people.

Dealing with sensory issues

Our five senses pick up information we need which is then processed by our brains before an appropriate response is enacted. The child (or adult) with autism may have either hypo (under sensitive) or hyper (over sensitive) senses which causes them to react in unusual ways.

A hypo reaction to the sense of balance may cause a child to rock, flap their hands, turn in circles, etc. This is because the child is not receiving enough information from their vestibular (balance) system to let them know where their body is in relation to their environment. A hyper reaction to the sense of balance might include experiencing car sickness or difficulty with physical activities such as sport. This is because the child's sense of balance is over sensitive and sends an overload of information.

Our bodies' proprioceptors tell us where we are in relation to other people or objects. Someone hyposensitive in this sense might bump into things or people. Someone with hypersensitivity in this sense might have difficulty with fine motor skills such as doing up buttons.

Olfactory (sense of smell) difficulties might cause a hyposensitive reaction where a person fails to detect smells or hypersensitive reaction where a person cannot tolerate certain smells.

Visual difficulties cause a hyposensitive response where the child's eyesight appears to be poor or blurred or hyper reaction where the child appears to notice tiny details or complains that bright lights 'jump' around.

Partial deafness, not acknowledging sounds or a liking for noise-making can be signs of a hypo auditory system. Hyper reactions might include an intolerance and dislike of crowds or being easily distracted.

Sensory difficulties with the tactile (or touch) receptors in the body might include hypo reactions of not feeling pain or wanting to feel pressure or tightness around the body. Hyper reactions might include dislike of certain fabrics against the skin or a dislike of being touched or hugged.

A child with hypo reactions to the sense of taste may eat unusual things. A child with a hyper sense of taste may only like smooth, plain foods.

'The child (or adult) with autism may have either hypo or hyper senses which cause them to react in unusual ways.'

Mum of Thomas, aged 10, says:

'Thomas is really sensitive to perfumes, so we try not to use them around him. This can be a problem for his older sister though. If people are wearing strong aftershaves, he will move away from them – even going into another room.

'The sound of other people eating is another problem for Thomas. Sometimes he won't eat with us. I have to take his food into another room so that he can eat there. Sometimes it is possible to have some background noise going on in the room like the TV and then he will sometimes stay at the table with us – but not always!'

The table below suggests ways of helping your child cope with hypo and hyper sensory issues.

Sensory system that deals with	Hypo (not enough)	Hyper (too much)
Balance	Use rocking horses and outside play equipment. Dance to music.	Avoid patterned flooring.
Body awareness	Place furniture and obstacles around sides of rooms. Teach your child to stand at arms length from people.	Create activities that develop fine motor control, e.g. playing with small Lego, pouring water from jugs into containers, dressing dolls with buttons, zips, etc.
Smell	Put one of your child's favourite smells onto a soft toy or piece of fabric. This might distract them from obsessions with smelling unpleasant things.	Use unscented products where possible. Avoid strong perfumes, deodorants, etc.
Sight	Use lots of visual stimulation such as strong colour, different lighting, brightness, etc.	Use sunglasses or Irlen coloured lenses. Use stick-on window shields in the car. Thick curtains and dim lighting are useful.
Sound	Have background music, a radio, etc. Play with musical instruments.	Use earplugs or an MP3 player in crowds. Close doors and windows if possible. Use 'ear defenders' (see the Sensory Processing Resource Centre website www.sensory-processing-resource.com).
Touch	Use weighted vests, weighted blankets or weighted lap pads. Some children like to be wrapped tightly in a blanket or have cushions placed on top of them.	Use light touch rather than hugs. Buy clothes made from fabrics your child can tolerate. Introduce new materials gradually.
Taste	Give your child something to eat or suck when around inedible objects/items that they lick or try to eat. Try Chewy Tubes for children who like to bite or chew things: www.kapitex.com.	Keep to plain and unspicy foods. Introduce new flavours and textures gradually.

Dealing with excessive stimming

Stimming is a self-stimulatory action that produces a feeling of security, relaxation or wellbeing in the person undertaking it. Stimming can be vocal (making noises, sniffing, throat clearing, etc) or physical (tapping, spinning, rocking, etc). Many people without autism have habits they engage in at times such as hair twirling, nail biting or doodling. The difference for the person with autism is that stimming can be an essential coping mechanism when they are in an anxiety provoking situation or an important way in which they unwind or de-stress.

It may be easy to recognise your child's particular stimming activities and you might feel that they do not usually cause particular problems. Occasionally, however, stimming can interfere with social interactions or even be dangerous. On these occasions, you need to find a way to divert your child's attention away from them. Distraction or encouraging your child to wait for a more appropriate time before stimming is the best approach. Unless your child's stimming is putting them or others in real danger, physically restraining the activity may only cause your child (and you) more distress.

An older child can be taught socially acceptable stimming. Some parents teach their child to use a degree of self-control, i.e. to stim later when at home, in private or when they have finished what they are doing.

'Stimming is a self-stimulatory action that produces a feeling of security, relaxation or wellbeing in the person undertaking it.'

Sensory rooms

A sensory room is a safe, stimulating and therapeutic environment for children (or adults) who have sensory processing difficulties. Hospitals, clinics or special schools often contain a lot of expensive and sophisticated equipment, but it is possible to make a sensory room in your own home. If you don't have a spare room then an area of an existing room will do just as well.

The website of the Sensory Processing Disorder Resource Center gives many useful and achievable tips for creating a safe and beneficial room or area for children with ASDs. The idea is to include equipment, objects and activities in the room that take account of your child's hypo or hyper sensitivities and that will stimulate and calm – whatever is needed.

Examples include:

- Soft, low lighting.
- Bubble or lava lamps.
- Scented soft toys.
- Weighted cushions or blankets for wrapping around the child.
- Hammocks for swinging in.
- Soft rocking horses or chairs.
- Tunnels for squeezing into.
- A trampoline.
- Toys to push or pull.
- Indoor wind chimes.
- CDs with natural sounds.
- Different textured fabrics.

Your knowledge of your child and your imagination will enable you to put together a room or area that your child will find soothing and therapeutic. The room can become a place where your child can calm down, use up excess energy or engage with their environment.

Summing Up

Use some of the ideas suggested in this chapter to make your home as autism friendly as possible. Parents have found that creating such an environment can be of great benefit to their child. When you have an environment that takes account of your child's sensitivities, you may find it has a good effect on your child's behaviour, reactions and ability to engage with others and their surroundings.

'When you have an environment that takes account of your child's sensitivities, you may find it has a good effect on your child's behaviour, reactions and ability to engage with others and their surroundings.'

Chapter Five

Interventions and Therapies

As the parent of a child with autism, you will naturally want to find the methods or interventions that could help them develop in all areas of their life. There are so many interventions, therapies and methods that claim to help children make progress towards reaching their full potential, and it can be difficult to know where to start. It can be a challenge to know which ones will benefit your child because every child with autism is different. A programme or method that works wonders with one child may have little or no effect on another child.

Interventions do not aim to cure autism. Their aim is to alleviate some of the difficulties children with autism experience with social interaction, behaviour or learning. They try to make the child's life easier and happier – as well as yours. Be wary of 'experts' who claim a particular intervention programme will cure your child's autism. Check with your child's GP and other professionals involved with their care and education. Ask their advice about appropriate methods that you could use to help your child.

'Check with your child's GP and other professionals involved with their care and education. Ask their advice about appropriate methods that you could use to help your child.'

What's involved?

- Time – yours and your child's. Many interventions need several sessions a day or a certain number of hours per week to give maximum benefit.

- Money – you may need to pay to go on training days to learn about the method or invest in books or DVDs that will teach you. You may also need to buy equipment.

- **Space** – you may need a room or area of your home to devote to the implementation of some interventions.

- **Qualified experts** – for some interventions you will need to take your child to an appropriately qualified and experienced practitioner, e.g. for music or speech therapy.

- **Energy and dedication** – you may be in for a long term effort.

- **Flexibility** – if the programme doesn't suit your child, you may need to adapt it or try something else.

- **Support** – make sure other family members and those who have contact with your child in a caring role know what you are trying to achieve and how so that they do not unwittingly undo your child's efforts and progress. This would be especially important with behavioural programmes or dietary interventions.

'It can be useful to speak to other parents who have used the strategies you may be thinking of trying.'

The following tables give brief summaries of some of the many strategies, interventions and programmes that parents have tried and found to be beneficial. Remember that your child is an individual. You know your child best and may be able to see immediately that some of these ideas will work and some will not. Find out all you can about those that sound as though they would benefit your child. It can be useful to speak to other parents who have used the strategies you may be thinking of trying.

The National Autistic Society website provides greater details on many of the following ideas. They also produce a very useful publication outlining interventions for autism and where to get further information – see *Approaches to Autism – An Easy To Use Guide To Many And Varied Approaches To Autism*.

The tables below divide the interventions into six areas:

- Behavioural or daily life strategies.

- Speech and language enhancing interventions.

- Special diet ideas.

- Social skills training.

- Complementary therapies.

- Drug intervention under medical supervision.

Behavioural and daily life strategies

Name	What it does	Possible benefits to child	Further info from
ABA or Applied Behavioural Analysis (sometimes called Lovass therapy)	Looks at the way a person's environment impacts on their behaviour.	One-to-one instruction at first, leading to group work when the child has learnt to cope with distraction. Builds skills in interaction, play. Behaviour management including aggression. Needs many hours a week/day for maximum benefit.	PEACH (Parents for the Early Intervention of Autism in Children), www. peach.org.uk.
PLAY or Play and Language for Autistic Youngsters	Parents are taught (via tutor or DVD) how to get their child to interact where they already are and to move them on to further interaction and engagement.	You become your child's play partner by joining them in what they are already doing and moving them on to further interaction.	Training DVD and full details available from www.playproject. org.
TEACCH	Structured activities within a highly structured and predictable environment. Child is given simple activities and encouraged to complete them. Uses picture symbols to help the child communicate. It is possible to adapt the method to use at home around routines.	Because the environment is very structured, the child knows what to expect and what to do which is reassuring for them. Encourages independence. Accommodates a child's autistic traits and is often used in special schools. Concerned with holistic or whole person development. Picture symbols help child to interact and remove frustration for non-verbal children.	www.teacch. com.

Daily Life Therapy	Residential day programmes that provide children with academic, physically active and group work activities and experiences.	A holistic approach that aims to help the child develop emotionally, socially and intellectually as far as possible.	Horizon School for Autism. See help list.
Social Stories™	Individually composed stories that teach or reinforce a message about social behaviour or that prepare a child for an approaching event.	The story takes account of the individual child's needs. The stories are not judgemental but are a way of nudging the child to think and act the right way.	www. thegraycenter. org or www. socialstories. com.
Neuro-therapy	Clinician places electrode magnetic sensors to the child's head which records the brain's reaction when the child watches certain stimuli via video games. Sensors beep and give reward points each time the child reacts in a desired state.	Helps to retrain the child's reactions to stimuli.	Association for Comprehensive Neuro-therapy, www.latitudes. org. Delacato Clinic UK, www. theautismcentre. co.uk.
Son-Rise	The parent is encouraged to initially 'join' the child in their activity/world in an accepting way before any behaviour modification is attempted. Parents are also supported and encouraged to explore their own feelings about their child.	One-to-one help. Going at child's own pace. Encourages bond between parent and child.	Information and training DVDs from the Autism Treatment Center of America, www.autism treatmentcenter. org.

Speech and language interventions

Name	What it is	Possible benefits to child	Further info from
Speech therapy	A speech therapist assesses your child's understanding and ability to use language. They provide an individualised programme to aid your child's skills in this area.	Usually one-to-one attention. Gains in social interaction can be made. Child's speaking and listening skills can improve greatly.	Your GP, school, other professional or Advisers on Autism at the Royal College of Speech and Language Therapists, www.rcslt.org.
Hanen – early language	A form of speech therapy where parent, therapist and child work together to help the child acquire and develop language skills.	The parent or carer carries out the programme once it has been taught to them. Can be individualised according to your child's needs.	Ask your child's speech therapist or visit The Hanen Centre, www.hanen.org.
Makaton	A form of communication that involves signing, language and facial expression. It links words and picture cards.	Parent's can learn the method and carry it out day to day. Can provide a non-verbal child with a method of communicating while verbal communication is acquired.	www.makaton.org.
The Listening Programme	Music trains the brain in auditory skills and improvement.	Helps the child's ability to discriminate background noise. Aids a child's hypo or hyper sensitivity to sound. Needs to be carried out by a trained practitioner.	www.learning-solutions.co.uk.
Picture Exchange Commun-Ications System (PECS)	Use of picture cards which the child points to in order to communicate needs, etc. Child progresses on to using pictures that convey more complex sentences.	Can be successful in enabling a non-verbal child to acquire communication skills.	Pyramid Educational Consultants, www.pecs.org.uk
Oral Motor Programme	Provided by a speech or occupational therapist. The goal is to develop positive and enjoyable use of the mouth by dealing with sensory awareness and discrimination.	Improves speech, tolerance of foods not previously tolerated, etc.	Ask your GP or your child's speech or occupational therapist about this. See also Therapy Shoppe, www.therapyshoppe.com.

Biochemical, allergy and nutrition programmes

Name	What it is	Possible benefits to child	Further info from
Immunity Improving Interventions	Diets that avoid certain additives, stimulants or certain products, e.g. milk. Or adding probiotics, essential fatty acids or inflammatory combating antitoxins (e.g. vitamins A, C, E).	Eliminates the side effects that cause adverse behavioural or health problems in children with autism due to the brain-gut connection. Adding particular supplements can boost the child's immune system.	Check with your child's GP before eliminating or adding products to their diet and before following any special diets. Allergy induced Autism, www.autismmedical.com.
Lead and mercury elimination	Avoiding exposure to heavy metal based products. These are believed to cause some dysfunction in the immune system of children who have autism, which in turn gives rise to their behaviours.	The belief is that the child's immune system is better regulated.	Check with your child's GP before giving medication that alters metabolism.
Diets – elimination of certain products	May be refined sugar, eggs, chicken, yeast products, processed foods, artificial colourings, artificial sweeteners or certain proteins such as monosodium glutamate.	Avoidance of allergic reactions in a child which may include headaches, dizziness eczema or breathing difficulties.	Consult your child's GP before changing your child's diet or experimenting with it. For further information on biomedical interventions see Autism Research Institute, www.autism.com. Click on 'treating autism' and then biomedical approach. Remember not to assume that methods that claim to cure will work with all children.
Diets – supplements	The addition of particular vitamins or minerals are introduced to their diet.	Child's diet deficiencies are rebalanced thus improving immune system and health.	Check with your child's GP before starting any supplements or changing your child's diet. Additional advice from Autism Management, www.autismmanagement.com.

Complementary therapies

Name	What it is	Possible benefits to child	Further info from
Aromatherapy and massage therapy	Aromatherapy can include use of fragrances as well as physical interactions that can help some children develop trust.	Development of non-verbal communication between parent and child. Multi sensory learning.	Read *Aromatherapy and Massage for People with Learning Difficulties* by H Sanderson and others.
Art therapy	Use of art and creative materials for therapeutic and communication purposes.	Provides an insight into the child's thoughts and interpretations. Enables non-verbal communication with the world outside of the child.	British Association of Art Therapists, www.baat.org.uk.
Auditory Integration Training or AIT	A retraining of the hearing that can enable people affected by autism and sound sensitivity to disregard intrusive sounds.	Can help a child cope with auditory sensitivities.	The National Light and Sound Therapy Centre in London, www.light-and-sound.co.uk.
Dance, drama and yoga	Dance, drama and yoga enable social situations to be tested and experienced.	Can help develop trust, interaction skills, creativity, feeling part of a group. Yoga can have strengthening and calming effects.	The British Association of Drama Therapists, www.badth.ision.co.uk. The Association of Dance Movement Therapy UK, www.admt.org.uk. For yoga see *Yoga for Children with Autistic Spectrum Disorders* by D and S Betts.
Reflexology	This works on the principle that pressure and massage of particular areas of the feet improve the functioning of the immune system.	As well as having a relaxing, calming effect on some individuals, it may help improve the functioning of the digestive and immune system.	www.footreflexology.com.

Social skills

Name	What it is	Possible benefits to the child	Further info from
Befriending	Organised through local groups by the National Autistic Society. Vetted volunteers are matched to families to be companions/ friends to people with autism.	Alleviates loneliness and enables child to develop social skills.	The National Autistic Society or your local branch if you have one. www.autism.org. uk/befriending.
School buddies scheme	The teacher matches and allocates volunteer classmates to befriend another child.	Child is less isolated in school environment.	Your child's school or teacher.
Social skills groups	Therapist or teacher supervises and supports children with special needs in small group sessions/activities.	A safe and controlled environment is created for children to interact and develop social skills.	Mental or health professionals dealing with your child, e.g. your GP, CAMHS, etc.
Social Stories™	Invented by Carol Gray. Individually composed stories that explore the child's social situations and suggest ways of behaving or reacting.	Can help prepare a child for different situations that they may otherwise find stressful or too difficult to do.	www.thegraycenter.org or www.socialstories. com.
Clubs, societies, groups, etc	Activities and groups run for children in your area that involve your child's interests.	Meeting others with the same interests. Development of social skills/ interaction.	Local directories, advertisements or library.
Pet therapy	Caring for and communicating with own chosen pet.	Can help child to de-stress and learn to think about 'someone' else's needs.	Dr Temple Grandin's book *Animals in Translation* is an interesting view of how those with autism may be able to relate to animals. Also see www.autism-spectrum-disorders. com.
Lego therapy	Developed by paediatric neuropsychologist Daniel LeGoff. Small group activity where children co-operate together to build Lego models.	Benefits child who can cope with small group of other children. Teaches interaction, social skills, team work, etc.	The Center for Neurological and Neurodevelopmental Health, www.thecnnh. org.

Drugs

Name	What it is	Possible benefits to child	Further info from
Medication and drug intervention	Medication that influences and controls behaviour under the recommendation and ongoing monitoring of a doctor only.	Can alleviate anxiety, extreme obsessive behaviour, aggression, depression, etc.	Your child's GP. The mental health charity MIND has information on autism and medication, www.mind.org.uk.

Tips from other parents

Finding interventions, activities and therapies that suit your child can make a huge difference to their development and behaviour, in turn making a difference to the whole family. You may find that a certain intervention can help you and your child tackle a wide variety of problems. In particular, common difficulties include toileting and toilet training, your child's ability to make themselves understood, getting your child to respond to you or others, inappropriate behaviour, loneliness or isolation, hygiene issues, sleep problems, tantrums and OCD.

As you investigate and develop different interventions for your own child, you might also like to consider the following tips offered by other parents of children with autism. See also chapter 7 which includes ideas for coping with issues with older children but may also be useful for younger children. Always remember that every child is different. An idea that may work well for one may not work at all with another.

'Finding interventions, activities and therapies that suit your child can make a huge difference to their development and behaviour, in turn making a difference to the whole family.'

Toilet training

- Develop a toileting routine that teaches each stage from communicating a need to use the toilet to leaving the bathroom afterwards.

- Make your bathroom as autism friendly as possible.

- Leave out the potty stage as this often makes the process more complicated for a child with autism – they may find it difficult to transfer the skill of using a potty to that of using a proper toilet. Use a special child toilet seat that attaches to the toilet instead.

- When your child is still in nappies, do the nappy changing in the bathroom so he/she associates this with this particular room.

- If possible, start the toilet training in the early summer as your child will probably be encumbered with less clothing.

- Use picture sequences to teach toilet training. Put the pictures in the bathroom and point out each stage/picture as you help your child to do them, e.g. getting clothes out of the way, sitting on the toilet.

- See each sequence through to the end even if your child doesn't do anything.

- Set regular times for going through the sequence.

- If your child is fearful of the toilet flushing sound then leave this until the sequence is finished and you are ready to leave the bathroom.

- If teaching a boy to urinate standing up, place a piece of tissue paper in the toilet for him to aim at.

- For a child who lacks awareness of sensation, teach them to go to the toilet at set times and to know when those times are. Also, teach them to remain on the toilet for a set length of time so that they do not get up too soon!

- For night time training use waterproof bedding. Get your child up to go to the toilet at least twice during the night.

- Check out the ERIC (Education and Resources for Improving Childhood Continence) website www.eric.org.uk for further ideas and information.

Communication and response

- Don't do everything for your child. If they need something they will have to find a way to communicate the need.

- Allow your child plenty of time to speak or communicate.

- Praise and reward efforts.

- Join in your child's play – this will give them interaction opportunities.

- Start a game/activity you know your child likes near to where they are. This may catch their interest and encourage them to join you and interact.

- Ask your child questions and give choices so they are required to indicate or state a preference.

- For a non-verbal child, investigate the use of voice output communication devices for some of the time (see www.abilitynet.org.uk).

- Use visual aids to help your child say what they want to say.

- Make topic folders. These can contain pictures or objects related to a particular subject and enables you to look at and talk about the particular thing together.

- Useful book: *Autism, Play and Social Interaction* by L Gammeltoft and M Sollock Nordenhof.

'Don't do everything for your child. If they need something they will have to find a way to communicate the need.'

Inappropriate behaviours

- Learn to spot what may develop into an inappropriate behaviour.

- Intervene early.

- Distract the child.

- As far as possible, explain why the behaviour is inappropriate, where it would be okay and what the child could do instead.

- If possible, suggest and provide acceptable alternatives that will fulfil the sensory purpose of the original behaviour, e.g. replace your child's desire to lick inappropriate objects by giving him/her a lolly to lick instead.

Encouraging integration

- Encourage communication as already described.

- Encourage your child to join a small group/club for children with similar interests if you think they will be able to cope with it and enjoy the time spent there.

- Set play dates with another parent and child and see if they get on. Organise structured, specific activities for them to do.

- Always respect your child's individuality. You cannot and should not force a child who dislikes the company of others to be sociable and join in. Just give them plenty of opportunities and encouragement.

- With an older child, use any local social skills groups for children with ASDs that there may be.

- Teach your child about appropriate behaviour around other people, e.g. sharing, talking and listening skills, appropriate and inappropriate touching of others.

- Draw 'stick men' speech and thought bubble pictures for explaining unwritten social rules. If you're feeling really creative, try making picture strip cartoons for your child that explain different social concepts. Many children with autism really like cartoon strip stories.

- Do not force your child to make actual eye contact with other people as many children with autism find this very uncomfortable and difficult.

Need2Know

Relationship circles

Relationship circles are an idea devised by different autism experts/teachers/writers and can be used to help your child understand how we respond appropriately to the different people we meet or know.

Draw the following to help your child understand different relationships:

In the centre of a piece of paper, draw a figure to represent your child. Draw a circle around the figure. Around this circle draw a second circle. Around the second circle draw a third circle. Around the third circle draw a fourth circle. Make the circles big enough so that you can write words or draw pictures representing other people inside them.

Now, in each circle write the following words (or draw a picture to represent the words):

Circle 1: 'People very close to me' – Mummy, Daddy, grandparents, brothers, sisters, very special friends.

Circle 2: 'People I know well' – other friends, other relatives, special teachers.

Circle 3: 'People I see a lot' – people at school, next door neighbours.

Circle 4: 'Strangers and people I don't really know' – the bus driver, shop keeper.

Tell your child that people in Circle 1 are those to whom we are closest. It is okay to tell them personal and private things. It is okay to hug or kiss them or for them to do this to us. People in Circle 2 usually share less personal things about each other, they might hug or kiss in a less intimate way. People in Circle 3 might shake hands. They don't share personal information. People in Circle 4 may just say 'hello' or, more usually, not speak unless there is a particular reason to do so, e.g. a stranger might ask you the way to the railway station.

Hygiene issues

- Explain why it is important to be clean.

- Find deodorants, soaps, washing powders that do not irritate your child's sensory systems.

- Teach hand washing before eating, after going to the toilet, etc.

- Useful book to read: *Taking Care of Myself* by Mary Wrobel.

Tantrums and difficult behaviour

- Remember that children with autism can become very frustrated when they cannot communicate or make themselves understood.

- Avoid unnecessary changes in routine which can lead to anxiety.

- Use visual supports if your child is non-verbal and encourage them to use them to let you know what the problem is.

- With an older/more able child, get them to use a stress indicator. The child indicates where on the scale their stress levels are. To make a stress indicator, draw something that looks a bit like a thermometer with a cut out arrow which the child can place on the scale to show where their stress levels are.

- Learn to recognise the early warning signs that your child is becoming stressed or frustrated.

- Identify sensory stimuli that may distress your child. You might need to avoid taking your child to places where noise, lights or smells cause an adverse reaction in your child.

- Use distraction techniques if it's not too late – this might include suggesting an activity that enables your child to be alone for a short while.

- If your child is severely distressed, do not wade in shouting at them. They will be unable to listen or rationalise what you are saying.

- Try to remove what is causing the behaviour or move your child away from it.

- Give your child some space and encourage others to do the same.

- If a tantrum involves another person, once the episode is over insist that apologies are made where apologies are due and explain why if necessary.

- If your child is able to understand, talk to them about emotions and why people react the way they do. Give examples of when things annoy or upset you and say how you might have reacted with anger but didn't. Explain what you did instead to help yourself.

- Use short, clear and precise sentences when talking to your child if they are behaving inappropriately. Be sure to make it clear that it is the behaviour that is unacceptable and not the individual child themselves.

- Useful book to read: *Challenging Behaviour and Autism* by Philip Whitaker.

Dad of Emma, aged eight:

'If possible, we try to ignore tantrums. When she has calmed down a bit we try to distract her. If she is having one of her throwing and lashing out tantrums, we remove anything sharp or dangerous from nearby. Emma can click back into normal very quickly once the tantrum is over. Her first words might even be "what's for dinner?"

'What definitely doesn't work is shouting back or trying to reason with her.'

'Remember that children with autism can become very frustrated when they cannot communicate or make themselves understood.'

Dealing with OCD

Remember that OCD is not the same as engaging in autism-type repetitive behaviour or a liking for rigid routines. It is an anxiety disorder and, in extreme cases, can lead a person into becoming unable to take part in everyday activities due to the development of intense and irrational fears. The obsession can be described as a preoccupation with a thought which the person believes to be threatening, or an irrational, negative thought. The 'compulsion' or 'compulsive behaviour' is the behaviour/ritual the person feels they need to do in order to relieve the anxiety caused by the negative thought or fear. Examples of OCD rituals are persistent hand washing, touching things a certain number of times or constant checking that something has been done.

It can be difficult and stressful for the whole family to cope with a child who has OCD. Parents often find that they are manipulated into carrying out some of the child's rituals. It can be hard to resist the child's demands because doing so can result in the child showing great stress as well as tears, tantrums and even aggression. What do other parents and professionals say you can do that will help your child?

- Intervene early if you can – as soon as you see OCD behaviour developing.

- Distract your child from engaging in the compulsive behaviour.

- Your child may be able to limit the time they spend on an OCD behaviour. Use a reward system if they manage this.

- Reward the child if/when they manage to resist the behaviour completely.

- Get specialist help and advice. Your GP may be able to refer your child for treatment for OCD. You could also see the advice given by the UK charity OCD Action at www.ocdaction.co.uk. Treatment or therapy for OCD includes a form of cognitive behaviour therapy called exposure and response prevention (ERP). This involves exposing the child to the very thing that they are scared of and then encouraging the child not to carry out the neutralising compulsion. This method is difficult for the child to do but enables them to learn that nothing terrible happens when they stop practising the compulsive behaviour. Anxiety relieving medication is also sometimes used under medical supervision.

'Treating OCD is about helping the child to feel more able to cope with stressful situations, rather than trying to take the stress out of their lives.'
Cheryll Meikle, OCD therapist.

'Jake was nine when his OCD got really out of control. The life of his whole family revolved around his obsession. Jake became terrified of going through doorways unless he could place a piece of string on the floor before stepping over it and through. His family ignored what they thought would be a passing phase but eventually it became almost impossible to get Jake to go anywhere or at least anywhere without letting him do his "string thing". His parents tried being firm and not allowing him to do it. They tried bribes and rewards if he managed to resist the behaviour. All their attempts resulted in Jake crying, screaming and kicking. Eventually, a specialist therapist worked with Jake to help him overcome his fear and obsession. It was a question of getting him to approach doorways without the string, getting him to put one foot across, take one step across and eventually step right across. It took Jake and his family several months of hard work and persistence before his fear finally went.'

Anxiety

Some older children who have higher functioning autism may see the link between their anxiety and their OCD behaviour. Some parents say their child can use a scale/chart that rates anxiety, showing when their anxiety might lead them to engage in the compulsive behaviour the most. You could help your child make a chart, showing what will happen each day and how their anxiety levels might change in different situations. Here is an example:

Approximate time	Activity	Anxiety rating out of 10
8am	Get on school bus	9
8.30am	Registration time	7
9am	Maths	2
9.45am	PE	8
10.45am	Break	9
11am	Computing	1
5pm	Homework time	9
6pm	Dinner time	6
7pm	Watch TV	1

Making such a chart might help you and your child think of strategies that could help them cope with the high anxiety times. For example, getting to the bus stop early so that your child can sit at the front/by the window if that reduces anxiety; talking together about what happens in registration if that helps; checking together that your child has the right PE kit and talking through what will happen; having somewhere to go or having something in particular to do at break time; reminding your child to always write down the homework, checking your child understands what to do and has a quiet, less distracting place to get it done. For some children, knowing which situations cause the most anxiety and putting coping strategies in place help reduce anxiety reactions such as OCD.

'For some children, knowing which situations cause the most anxiety and putting coping strategies in place help reduce anxiety reactions such as OCD.'

Sleep problems

- Establish a bedtime routine.

- Ensure your child's bedroom is sleep inducing and autism friendly.

- Make sure the bedding is comfortable for your child. Try weighted blankets.

- Use Social Stories™ to explain why sleep is important.

- Play calming music at bedtime.

- Use rewards for 'good sleeping' on waking in the morning, e.g. stickers, favourite breakfast.

- Eliminate daytime naps and adjust bedtimes.

- Keep a sleep diary to show your child's GP or counsellor should sleep problems become more of an issue.

- If you are suffering from exhaustion because of your child's sleep disorder, make sure you get breaks, support or even respite – ask your social services about this.

- Two useful books to read: *Sleep Better! A Guide to Improving Sleep for Children with Special Needs* by V Mark Durand and *My Child Won't Sleep: Practical Advice and Guidance on the Common Sleeping Problems of Young Children* by J Douglas and N Richman.

How to write a social story

Parents and teachers have probably been using social stories of kinds for centuries, but Carol Gray describes a particular way of using an individually created story to teach your child how to manage or cope with certain situations. Her website www.socialstories.com describes the special way in which that is done.

The word 'story' is misleading as they are usually a series of short sentences that give a clear message about a situation, event or people. They might help a child understand things: why do I need to have my hair washed? Why should I try not to stare at people? What will happen if I run out into the road?

If you think your child could benefit from Social Stories™ you could try writing one and bear in mind the following tips:

- The story should not order or boss your child around.

- Don't describe how your child will feel in the story – this would only be a guess and you might be wrong.

- Use positive language and avoid negativity.

- Write the story from first or third person perspective.

- Use these four basic sentence types: descriptive ('On Saturdays Tom usually goes swimming'), perspective ('Tom can feel cold when he gets out of the swimming pool', affirmative ('It is a clever idea to dry with a towel when you get out of the swimming pool. This is a good idea') and directive ('Tom will try to remember to dry himself with the towel really well').

- Illustrate your story. You could type it on the computer and download pictures to slot in to it (see, for example, www.sparklebox.co.uk).

- The National Autistic Society Help2 programme for parents includes a seminar on how to write these stories. These seminars are held in various locations in the UK. See their website for more details (found in the help list).

'A social story is a particular way of using an individually created story to teach your child how to manage or cope with a certain situation.'

Summing Up

Investigating the many interventions and strategies that have helped other children affected by autism will enable you to find methods that may help your own child. Remember to seek professional advice before embarking on a particular programme of therapy. Once you have found what works well for your child then make sure your partner/other family members/child's teacher/carer all support your efforts. Remember to enjoy your child's unique personality, strengths and abilities. Show your child that you value them for who they are and that your focus is not all on coping with the things they find difficult.

'Remember to enjoy your child's unique personality, strengths and abilities.'

Chapter Six

Education

Many children with ASDs attend mainstream pre-school or school. They tend to be at the higher functioning end of the spectrum with less profound or no additional learning difficulties. Attempts might be made to integrate children who are more severely affected by autism, or who have additional problems, into mainstream settings and sometimes the adjustments that can be made to meet their needs are enough. Sometimes their special needs are not best met in this way.

Many children with autism are unable to manage in ordinary nurseries or schools and may either attend special units attached to schools or go to special schools. However, some parents feel that their child's needs are not adequately catered for at school at all and choose to 'home-school' their child.

This chapter looks in a very basic way at the possible educational options for children affected by autism in the UK.

Pre-school provision

This includes pre-schools or playgroups for two to five-year-olds, nursery schools and nursery classes in schools. Pre-school provision is provided by the state or is offered by privately owned pre-school providers.

Day nurseries cater for children from a few months old to age four or five. They usually provide all-day care throughout the year and are useful for parents working full-time as their days are longer than the average school day.

'Attempts might be made to integrate children who are more severely affected by autism, or who have additional problems, into mainstream settings and sometimes the adjustments that can be made to meet their needs are enough.'

Between the ages of two and three, children embark on the foundation stage of the curriculum. Their learning experiences and activities are geared towards six areas of learning: language, communication and literacy; mathematics; knowledge and understanding of the world; personal, social, emotional and spiritual development; creative development; physical development.

Various considerations need to be made when introducing a child with autism to the pre-school setting:

- Do the staff have knowledge, training or experience of ASDs?

- The child will need a very gradual introduction to the setting: perhaps a first visit when there are no other children present followed by short stays with the parent/carer remaining at first.

- A staff member allocated to greeting and caring for the child throughout the session is ideal – as with the key worker staff scheme which many nurseries employ.

- Staff need to be aware of and support interventions and strategies that the parents employ with the child.

- If the child is non-verbal then a scheme needs to be in place so that the child and staff can communicate with each other, e.g. pictures, labels, etc.

- The setting's special educational needs co-ordinator (SENCO) will need to compile the child's Individual Education Plan (IEP). This is done after consultation with parents (and perhaps professionals involved in the child's care, e.g. a speech therapist). The purpose of the IEP is to ensure that the special needs of the child are taken into account and that the curriculum is adjusted or supplemented in order to better fulfil those needs.

'Pre-school staff need to be aware of and support interventions and strategies that the parents employ with the child.'

Mainstream school education

Most children with autism need extra support if they are able to attend a mainstream school – whether the school is state run or private. Each local education authority (LEA) follows guidelines about how children are assessed and what special needs support is available. As this can vary throughout the UK, it is necessary to consult your child's teacher, school or your local education authority for how this is done in your area.

There are various levels of support depending on the severity of the child's difficulties. The levels (or equivalents) are:

- Initial Action.
- School Action (Early Years Action for pre-school aged children).
- School Action Plus (Early Years Action Plus for pre-school aged children).
- Statement of Special Educational Needs.

If it is very obvious that your child has quite profound needs that affect their learning then the request, consisting of information and evidence put together by the school, yourself and any professional involved in your child's wellbeing, will probably be made fairly quickly. Higher functioning children with autism and perhaps those with Asperger's syndrome often receive no more additional support than that offered at the Initial Action or School Action stages.

Whatever special provision is eventually agreed and provided, it will be monitored regularly and adjustments will be made as your child develops or as any new problems arise. If your child is statemented then the whole statement is reviewed annually at a special meeting which you, your child's teacher(s) and any relevant/helpful professionals (e.g. an educational psychologist) attends.

Special provision and statements include details of what extra professionals may be involved in helping/teaching your child, e.g. speech therapist, specialist autism workers, etc. It will outline what short term and long term targets will be made and whether any special equipment or learning resources will be needed.

'Special provision and statements include details of what extra professionals may be involved in helping/ teaching your child, e.g. speech therapist, specialist autism workers, etc.'

England, Scotland, Wales and Northern Ireland have different procedures and planning methods for special needs children. The National Autistic Society publishes some useful leaflets and information on its website (www.autism.org.uk). This includes information and advice on:

- Choosing a school.

- Types of provision in different parts of the UK.

- Advocacy for parents and mediation.

- Moving from primary to secondary.

- Disability discrimination.

- Coping with the classroom environment.

- Coping with break and lunch times.

- Educational legislation.

- Resources on education and educational provision for children with autism.

If you do not agree with the type of provision being made for your child, you can contact a Parent Partnership or mediation service. These (or whatever is equivalent in your area) are provided free of charge by the Department for Children, Schools and Families (DCSF).

Once your child reaches 14 and is in school then a Transition Plan may be made. It will make suggestions about future schooling, college, training, getting work and support needed. A Transition Plan can continue until the young person is aged 25.

The organisation Oaasis has a useful website that has information on special educational needs and also a helpline for parents and professionals. Oaasis is a free information organisation for anyone caring for a child affected by an ASD or other disabilities. Their information sheets include one on finding a special needs school and another on dealing with exams (see help list for details).

Special units and special schools

Some children on the spectrum are not best catered for in mainstream school and so attend special units. These may be for children with a variety of needs or just for children with ASDs. Some children will remain in the special unit all day while others will access some of the classes and provision in the main school at certain times or on certain days.

The advantage of the units is that the child's needs are better met in an environment that takes account of such problems like sensory sensitivities or behavioural difficulties. The child can receive both small group and one-to-one teaching and often specialist therapy as well. The opportunity to join with the main part of the school is there for pupils who are able to benefit from this.

You can express a preference for your child to attend a particular mainstream maintained school or type of special school. The LEA must make a case that the school will not best benefit your child if they do not agree. You may also make representation for an independent or non-maintained school. In the case of independent education, this will make a difference as to who will pay the fees.

The Advocacy for Education Service offers parents advice and information about finding and getting the schooling they would like for their child (see help list).

'Special schools may cater for just children with autism or for children with a variety of special needs.'

Home schooling

Another option, which many parents like and find works well, is home schooling.

Both the Education Act (England and Wales) 1996 and the Education Act (Scotland) 1980 state that parents have a duty to provide their children with suitable education in a school setting or by other means. 'Other means' allows for home schooling.

Parents can decide to home educate for numerous reasons. When the child has autism, the reasons may include being better able to tailor learning experiences to the child's capabilities and interests, being better able to accommodate the child's hyper or hypo sensitivities, being able to fit educational learning in with any special interventions the child may be having and protecting the child from bullying and social situations which they find difficult to cope with.

As with all parents who decide to home educate, you will need to consider how you can provide an adequate curriculum long term, how you will meet your child's social needs and how your child will prepare and take any public examinations later on.

A useful book for parents is *Home Educating Our Autistic Spectrum Children: Paths Are Made By Walking* by T Dowty and K Cowlishaw.

Points to remember when home schooling

If your child has a Statement of Special Educational Needs, the SEN Code of Practice (Code of Practice, 2001, section 8:95) states that:

'...it remains the LEA's duty to ensure that the child's needs are met. The statement must remain in force and the LEA must ensure that parents can make suitable provision, including provision for the child's special educational needs. If the parents' arrangements are suitable, the LEA are relieved of their duty to arrange the provision specified in the statement. If, however, the parents' attempt to educate the child at home results in provision which falls short of meeting the child's needs, then the parents are not making "suitable arrangements" and the LEA could not conclude that they were absolved of their responsibility to arrange the provision in the statement. Even if the LEA is satisfied, the LEA remains under a duty to maintain the child's statement and to review it annually.' (Extract © Crown copyright 2001 Department for Education and Skills, now Department for Children, Schools and Families).

Rules may differ depending where in the UK you live, so it is important to check what rules are in place in your area.

However, if your child is not yet of school age then you may be able to begin home schooling without informing your LEA. However, if they become aware, you will need to provide evidence of the suitable provision you are providing.

If you decide to remove your child from school in order to begin home schooling, make sure you ask the school to remove your child's name from the register as this will avoid the problem of assumed absenteeism.

If your child is at a special school and you decide to remove them in order to home educate, you should ask your LEA's permission. You can contact the secretary of state for education if they do not agree.

Tips for the classroom

Teachers who have a child with autism in their class need to remember that this child will see and interpret the world in different ways to neuro-typical people and will, therefore, react and respond differently to many things.

Remember:

- Children with autism may interpret language literally.

- Children with autism may need instructions broken down or repeated.

- They may need instructions addressed to the whole class repeated to them personally.

- They may not apply knowledge acquired in one situation to another situation, i.e. they do not generalise.

- They tend to compartmentalise their learning, e.g. eating can only be done in a certain place.

- They have hypersensitivities which may mean they cannot cope with noise, crowds, bright lights and distracting sounds.

- They may engage in unusual repetitive behaviours that enable them to cope with their hypersensitivities.

- They may have hyposensitivities which may mean they engage in self-stimulatory activities such as hand flapping, finger flicking or rocking.

- They are often vulnerable to bullying or teasing.

- They benefit from consistency, routines and adherence to timetables. They may need to be given time to process an answer if asked a question and they may understand abstract ideas better when visual aids are used.

'Teachers who have a child with autism in their class need to remember that this child will see and interpret the world in different ways to neuro-typical people and will, therefore, react and respond differently to many things.'

Homework – a parent's tips

Mum of Daniel, aged 11:

'Homework can be a nightmare! We always set a time to do this and stick to it – for example, Saturday morning at 11.00. I give Daniel warnings before it gets to 11.00 so he is prepared for homework time. You need to find somewhere where there will be no distractions or interruptions as far as possible. Make sure the rest of the family know they can't interrupt you while you supervise your child with their homework. Get everything prepared that they are going to need like rulers, books, etc. I always start by making sure Daniel understands what he has to do. You can break things down into steps or write down a short plan and cross off each bit as it is done. We always have a treat ready for Daniel when he has done the homework – bribes can help! I try to keep calm because I've learnt that not keeping calm and ending up yelling at him to just concentrate and get on with it only results in him doing less or maybe nothing at all.'

'Make sure the rest of the family know they can't interrupt you while you supervise your child with their homework.'

A parent.

Summing Up

Deciding what kind of schooling or educational provision is right for your child with autism may not be easy. It is important to consider all viable options and visit the schools and settings in which you think you may be interested. Ask the advice of professionals who may already be involved in your child's care or treatment. If possible, speak to other parents of children with autism to gain ideas and insights into the types of provision available near you. Remember that your child may require different types and amounts of support as they develop. If a type of schooling that works initially begins to seem less appropriate as your child gets older, rethink the options.

A useful book on children with special needs and their education is *Special Educational Needs – A Parent's Guide* (Need2Know).

'Remember that your child may require different types and amounts of support as they develop. If a type of schooling that works initially begins to seem less appropriate as your child gets older, rethink the options.'

Chapter Seven

Adolescence and Beyond

It can be a worrying time when your child reaches the teenage years and early adulthood. Your concerns can include what your child will be able to do on leaving school, how your child will cope with the physical and emotional changes of growing up, what kind of independence they will be able to achieve and, perhaps now more than ever, what the future will hold for them in the long term.

It can take a lot of preparation and effort to prepare a young person with autism for early adulthood, and the extra difficulties experienced at this stage can place added strain on parents and the family. Making sure you have your support network around you and access to good advice that suits you and your child's needs is essential.

Areas of concern at the adolescent stage might be about:

- College or training courses.
- Work.
- Growing up physically and emotionally.
- Relationships.
- Acquiring some independence.
- Long term future care and plans.

College and training courses

What your child does when they finish compulsory age schooling will depend on their individual abilities and interests. Some children with high functioning autism and Asperger's syndrome do, of course, move on to further and higher education and often achieve very high levels of academic success or qualifications. For others, and for those at the mid to lower end of the autism spectrum, different options may need to be looked at. Children in school who have a Statement of Special Educational Needs will usually have a Transition Plan made out for them. This will be put together by your child's school with the input of teachers, you and any specialists who have been involved in the care/education of your child.

If your child has an area of special interest and ability, e.g. computers, mathematics or art, then you could investigate full or part-time college courses in those subjects. Some teenagers on the spectrum are able to cope with ordinary college environments to some extent, provided they receive the right amount of support and mentoring. By now you will know what kind of environment your child can cope with and what level of support they are likely to need.

'Some teenagers on the spectrum are able to cope with ordinary college environments to some extent, provided they receive the right amount of support and mentoring.'

For many teenagers with autism, the barriers to coping with further or higher education are too great and so specialist courses in day or residential autism friendly environments may be a good option for them. The National Autistic Society's quarterly magazine *Communication* has advertisements and information about some of these day or residential colleges. You will need to get information about any you might be interested in and visit them to decide if they would be right for your child. Parents choose the residential option for different reasons. The advantages of these colleges are that staff will be trained and experienced in dealing with and teaching people with autism. They will understand your child's sensory sensitivities and behaviours and may use special teaching or learning or behaviour management techniques or strategies that benefit people with autism. Some parents feel no longer able to cope with the increasingly complex needs of their teenager. In the UK, Cambian schools and colleges run by Cambian Education are one organisation that offer specialist year-round care and education for young people with autism – some up to the age of 30.

Students taking a higher education course may be able to apply for Disabled Students' Allowances (see www.direct.gov.uk/DisabledPeople/EducationAndTraining). Financial aid is also available for eligible students who have disabilities and who want to take Open University courses.

How successful this stage will be for your child will depend on a number of things:

- Whether your child receives the right kind of support.

- Whether your child can cope with the environment.

- Their interest and motivation.

Think creatively and originally about how to get your child what they need, e.g. trying short part-time training courses with flexible hours or distance learning courses that can be taken as slowly (or as quickly) as required.

Work

Getting into employment at any age or stage in life can be challenging for someone with autism; there may be many barriers to finding and getting a job or developing a career. Whether or not they manage to achieve this will depend on a number of factors: the severity of the person's autism and communication difficulties, any additional learning disabilities the person may have, interests and motivation, support and opportunity.

Young people with higher functioning autism and Asperger's syndrome may have less difficulty or may have different problems. They may find ways to compensate for these – although it is also true that their intelligence and awareness of their differences and difficulties can cause them other stresses and problems. But how can you help your youngster more severely affected by autism get into the world of work?

It is true that a lot of adults with autism are either underemployed or unemployed for much or most of their lives. But every person with autism is different and so parents should not be put off from investigating and encouraging realistic possibilities for their child. Possible ways into the working world for those with moderate to more severe autism might include the following:

- Part-time voluntary work experience.

- Routine jobs that stay the same, e.g. packing, shelf filling.

- Working in family/parent's own businesses.

'Getting into employment at any age or stage in life can be challenging for someone with autism; there may be many barriers to finding and getting a job or developing a career.'

- Developing an interest into a self-employed business – no matter how small or inviable sounding!

- Working from home.

Make use of the National Autistic Society's Prospects Employment scheme if it operates in your area (www.autism.org.uk, search for 'prospects employment'). You can also read the National Autistic Society's online information about finding employment for people with autism, search under their A–Z directory.

Being employed can give adults (with or without autism) a sense of purpose and achievement. It enables a person to put their skills and abilities to use and to develop these further. It enables independence and enhances self-esteem and confidence. Parents of young people without autism would not encourage their offspring to go into jobs for which they are not suited or in which they would underachieve or have no interest. Therefore, parents, carers or professionals guiding young people with autism should not expect them to settle for such work either if they are capable of achieving more. Basic or low level jobs are a good stepping stone to more meaningful or satisfying employment and enable youngsters to develop the skills they need in order to cope in the work environment. If your child has the capability and desire to move into a more challenging job (assuming this is actually realistic), as parents you can do much to support and encourage. You could:

'If your child has the capability and desire to 'get on', i.e. to get a perceived better job, then (assuming this is actually realistic) as parents you can do much to support and encourage.'

- Encourage your young adult to keep developing their social and communication skills.

- Encourage them to realistically identify their abilities and develop their strengths.

- Build up their self-esteem and confidence – show them that you believe in them.

- Help them with finding suitable job opportunities.

- Investigate supported or sheltered employment opportunities in your area.

The Council for Disabled Children

This organisation aims to promote the participation of children and young people with disabilities. It runs many projects including:

- Extending inclusion – making it possible for children with special needs/ disabilities to take part in extended school and children's centre activities.

- Transition to adulthood – raising awareness of the needs of young people with special needs who are in their teens or twenties.

Growing up – physically and emotionally

Coping with changes

Growing up is a trying time for most teenagers and their parents. But when the young person has autism to contend with as well as hormonal and physical changes, adolescence can be even more of a challenging time.

Children with ASDs tend to be less emotionally developed than neuro-typical children, so when your teenager's peers are becoming interested in fashion, the opposite sex and independence, they will be leaving your youngster behind in these respects. Even high functioning and Asperger's youngsters may not become interested in such things as intimate relationships until they are into their twenties or, if they are interested, lack the social skills to achieve one. They will, however, notice that their peers are forming such relationships.

You may suddenly see all kinds of differences between your child and their neuro-typical peers that were not apparent before, and it can be upsetting for parents to see yet another aspect to their child that is not developing 'normally'.

It is best to prepare your child for the changes that their body will go through before they get to the stage at which this happens. Otherwise they may become alarmed at what is happening to their bodies. While less emotionally and socially mature, many children with ASDs begin the physical changes of puberty at an earlier than average age. How you go about preparing and explaining will depend on where on the spectrum your child is. Higher functioning children may be willing to read books aimed at them and you could discuss issues together. More severely affected youngsters need clear and simple facts, and non-verbal youngsters will need their usual way of communicating their questions and concerns to you, e.g. signing, using picture symbols or computer programmes.

Seizures

Some children with autism begin suffering from seizures when they reach puberty. These can be quite small and difficult to spot or more obvious and quite alarming. They occur because of the effect of hormonal changes. If your child begins to suffer from these, consult your GP for advice and treatment.

Hygiene

'If you notice changes in your child's behaviour and think it may be due to depression, make sure you seek medical help.'

Health and hygiene issues will also be of concern at this stage. You will need to teach your child how and how often to use deodorants and (for girls) how to use feminine hygiene products. Staying clean and odour free by showering, bathing and changing clothes may not be natural concerns for your child, but teaching routines that deal with these issues can work. Write the routine down in words (or in pictures if necessary) and put these instructions where your child needs them, like in the bedroom or bathroom. Get your child to practise the routines until they are familiar with them.

Useful books to read on this subject include *Taking Care of Myself: A Hygiene, Puberty and Personal Curriculum for Young People with Autism* by Mary Wrobel and *1001 Great Ideas for Teaching and Raising Children with Autism Spectrum Disorder* by Ellen Notbolm and Veronica Zysk.

Sex education

When it comes to sex education, try to find out what your child is being taught at school. Most schools give parents some notice via a letter home explaining when this topic is going to be dealt with. This will give you the chance to talk to your child first if you want to, or at least be prepared to answer any questions they might have.

Where your teenager is on the spectrum and your assessment of their ability to understand will influence how much you discuss with your child at different ages. Suitable books to use with children on the spectrum or with other special needs include: *Talking Together About Growing Up: A Workbook for Parents of Children with Disabilities* and *Talking Together About Sex and Relationships: A Practical Resource for Schools and Parents Working with Young People with Disabilities* both by Lorna Scott and Lesley Kerr-Edwards.

Even if you feel your adolescent is unlikely to develop an intimate relationship during their late teens or even later than that, he or she needs to know the facts. Like neuro-typical children, they need to know in order to understand feelings or desires they might have or develop later, to make more sense of physical changes in their own bodies and to keep themselves safe.

Depression

During the teenage years, youngsters with autism can be vulnerable to depression. This may be partly due to them becoming more aware of the differences in themselves compared with their peers. Other reasons can include bullying, frustration at being unable to make themselves understood or loneliness. Signs of depression that can be spotted in neuro-typical youngsters might include losing or gaining weight, isolating themselves, avoiding certain situations, not sleeping or sleeping too much, giving up activities or interests, quietness or withdrawal. A person with autism may behave in some or all of these ways anyway, so it can be difficult to know if they are becoming depressed. If you notice changes in your child's behaviour and think it may be due to depression, make sure you seek medical help.

When prescribed under medical supervision, medication can relieve the symptoms of depression that leave people unable to function as they normally would. Various types of counselling can be beneficial for youngsters at the higher functioning end of the spectrum and those who are able to engage in it. These are natural and sensible steps to take for anyone suffering in this way and are not a sign of failure.

Adolescence is often a time of turbulence and change that can be hard to adjust to – it is not surprising that many young people suffer from anxiety disorders or depression at this stage in their lives. Having to cope with the difficulties that autism causes on top of these changes can make life even more difficult.

Suggestions by other parents of adolescents with ASDs for promoting good mental health and self-esteem include:

- Banning the negative talk about autism – talk your child 'up' not 'down' to other people and to them.

- Allowing them to develop their special interests – it might be a job/career area.

- Getting plenty of fresh air.

- Finding a form of exercise they enjoy and can do. Swimming can be especially beneficial for those not fearful of water. Being physically active is good for mental health as it releases chemicals called endorphins which produce a good mood or feel-good feeling.

- Encouraging your child to continue to communicate feelings.

- Using Social Stories™ to help your child work out how to deal with difficult situations. (Social Stories™ can be used with adolescents and adults as well.)

- Continuing to encourage your child to form friendships or join groups that might interest them. This can help deal with loneliness.

If you think your adolescent is becoming depressed then talk to your GP. Your child might be referred to your local Child and Mental Health Service (CAMHS) where there are psychologists or counsellors who are experienced in helping children and teenagers with or without autism. Contact the National Autistic Society helpline for information too (see help list).

A useful book to read is *Revealing the Hidden Social Code* by M Howley and E Arnold.

Oaasis (the free information organisation for parents and carers of children and adolescents affected by autism or other disabilities) has information guides on dealing with issues such as anxiety, inappropriate behaviours, social skills and stranger danger tips. These information guides can be viewed online (see help list). For more information and advice, see *Depression – The Essential Guide* (Need2Know).

Relationships

The teenage years are a time when relationships become very important to young people. For many neuro-typical youngsters, this is the time when close friendships and intimate relationships occur. For the adolescent with autism, this is not likely or far less likely to occur. While neuro-typicals are able to use their naturally developed ability to form relationships, a person with autism is more likely to struggle even more at this stage and be left behind.

Some young people with autism do not want intimate relationships now or in the future. Others do want one but do not know or understand how to go about achieving this. As at earlier stages in your child's life, it can be distressing to see them becoming lonely or frustrated at their inability to make and maintain friendships which they may well want.

What can you do to help your adolescent cope with people and friendships at this stage? The following strategies may be useful:

- If your attempts at encouraging your child to join groups have been successful in the past, encourage them to keep going or to find new ones.

- Your child may benefit from meeting other youngsters on the spectrum, e.g. at special groups or by inviting another parent and their child round and getting to know them.

- Keep working on the strategies you use to help your child learn about appropriate behaviours in social situations. Use visual aids, Social Stories™ or role play to explain and practise situations.

- Don't force your child to have large numbers of friends – often just one or two are enough.

- Your child might enjoy the company of adults rather than other teenagers.

- Explain about your child's autism and difficulties to other teenagers who spend time with them.

- Don't expect too much of your child. Allow them to be themselves and respect their need for solitude.

- When supervised by parents and used with care, some online social networks can provide friendship too.

Many parents of adolescents on the spectrum worry that their child's lack of understanding may get them into difficulties or even danger if they come across people who may take advantage of them. Worries are about the young person being persuaded to get involved in activities such as trying drugs, getting drunk, getting involved in criminal activities or allowing someone to physically abuse them. A teenager with an ASD may not know how to get themselves out of a situation they do not want to be in and may not know how to ask for help. It is natural for parents to feel even more protective of their child at this stage. Make sure they know how to keep themselves safe by:

'Explain about your child's autism and difficulties to other teenagers who spend time with them.'

- Staying with friends you both know and trust.

- Knowing which behaviours are acceptable and which aren't.

- Knowing how to ask for help and to tell you (or someone else they trust) if they are worried about anything that is happening/has happened to them.

- Knowing how to put emergency plans into action for themselves (if capable), e.g. using a mobile phone to contact you or others who can help them if they are in a difficult situation, or by understanding how to use public transport so they can get home if stranded/lost.

Chantal Sicile-Kira, in her book *Adolescents on the Autism Spectrum*, talks about teaching young people with autism about personal safety, e.g. how to recognise when they need to say 'no' or 'go away!' Her book also deals with dating and intimate relationships which some older high functioning adolescents on the spectrum may develop.

Encouraging independence

Some children with ASDs gain more independence than others. You will need to judge what type and how much independence is appropriate and manageable for your own child. The following points are suggestions for encouraging the child who is capable of trying to be more independent:

- Encourage your child to try strategies that may enable them to control their own behaviour, e.g. when they get angry, they could try going to a quiet place or counting to 10.

- Let your child try doing things for themselves when they show signs of wanting to do this for the first time.

- Suggest your child tries doing a task for themselves that you or others might have always done in the past, e.g. polishing their own shoes (and knowing when they need doing) or cutting their own nails. Break the new task down into small steps to teach them their new skills.

- If your child tries something new and fails, don't show disapproval or upset. Make light of any mistakes. This teaches them that mistakes and failure are a normal and acceptable part of life, and doesn't mean people can't try again. Tell your child about things you find difficult or can't do.

- Don't always check that your child has done things you know they need to do, e.g. getting a school bag organised and packed the night before or remembering to wash their hair. Sometimes it is a good idea to allow them to forget or leave things undone. If they start complaining about the consequences, they will be more likely to realise the importance of remembering and doing these activities next time.

- Teach your child to manage their own sensory sensitivities. For example, if they don't like noise on train journeys, they should remember to take their ear plugs. If bright lights bother them, they should remember their sunglasses. Make visual reminders/lists for your child to look at that will help them remember what they need.

- Depending on your child's ability and understanding, allow them to help or do tasks in the home, e.g. loading and/or putting on the washing machine, planning or cooking a meal or deciding what you need on a shopping trip. Again make visual reminder lists or use Social Stories™ to help with this.

Praise your child for all their efforts and all their successes.

Some useful resources

The following websites are useful places to look for information and advice for your adolescent:

- www.raisinghorizons.com – There are sections that deal with different issues and cover age ranges from five to 19. The Teenage Years CD with parents' handbook helps young people develop strategies for coping with social situations.

- www.after16.org.uk – a website for young people and carers/parents. It has resources for disabled teenagers who are leaving school and includes information on money matters, further education and work.

In addition, K Dunn Baron has written some useful books for children on the autistic spectrum: *When My Autism Gets Too Big: A Relaxation Book for Children with Autistic Spectrum Disorders* and *The Incredible 5-point Scale: Assisting Children with Autism Spectrum Disorders in Understanding Social Interactions and Controlling Their Emotional Responses*.

Another useful title is *Challenging Behaviour and Autism: Making Sense, Making Progress* by P Whitaker and others. This is a guide to preventing and managing challenging behaviour for parents and teachers.

'Where the consequences can be managed, it is absolutely essential to allow mistakes to be made'.

Sheila Coates.

Planning for the future

Depending on the severity of your child's autism and your child's long term prognosis, you may have particular concerns about the future. Many parents worry about what will happen to their child when they are no longer able to look after them or when they are no longer around.

If you have other children then it is important not to overload them with a sense of responsibility for the sibling with autism. It is not the job or responsibility of your other children to take care of their brother or sister in the future. If they do so at some point then this must be their own choice.

There are various steps you can take to ensure that your child with autism will be looked after or that there will be people looking out for them in the future. These steps might include:

- Getting legal advice.

- Making a will that includes details of what you want for your child's care.

- Having an agreement with a relative, close family member or godparent to be your child's guardian.

- Getting any plans or agreements down in writing.

- Having money set aside in a special needs trust and appointing a trustee for your child's future.

- Finding out about Lasting Powers of Attorney together when your child becomes 18. You could also investigate how to appoint an advocate for your child.

- Getting information or advice from the Office of the Public Guardian at www.publicguardian.gov.uk.

- Downloading and reading *A Guide to the Mental Capacity Act 2005* by J Butcher (National Autistic Society, 2007). See www.autism.org.uk/mentalcapacityact.

Summing Up

As your child approaches and goes through adolescence, there will be many new challenges and difficulties to face. Don't try to tackle difficult problems on your own and remember that your GP, your child's teachers and others involved in your child's care can all help to support and advise at this stage. Celebrate your child's achievements and abilities with them as this will enhance their self-esteem and self-belief. It will go a long way in helping them reach their own individual full potential.

'Celebrate your child's achievements and abilities with them as this will enhance their self-esteem and self-belief. It will go a long way in helping them reach their own individual full potential.'

Chapter Eight

Benefits and Entitlements

This chapter takes a brief look at some of the benefits, allowances and concessions available to children with disabilities and their parents/carers. Whether you feel you are in need of any particular benefit or allowance will depend partly on the severity of your child's autism, any co-morbid condition they might have and your own personal and financial situation. Always check the eligibility criteria of any allowance or benefit and get up-to-date information from the organisations (your local authority, for example) that deal with particular entitlements.

Disability Living Allowance

This benefit is available for children and adults who need a lot of additional help and support with daily living due to disability – either mental or physical. Many children with autism have physical difficulties in addition to their autism and so this allowance may apply to them. The eligibility criteria are that the child is over three months old and needs extra help or looking after, or over three years with walking difficulties, or over five years and needing a lot of extra help to get out and about. The allowance helps with the cost of the extra care or to help with the expenses of getting around. The range of entitlement depends on individual circumstances. Information can be found on the Department for Work and Pensions website – see www.dwp.gov.uk.

'Disability Living Allowance is available for children and adults who need a lot of additional help and support with daily living due to disability.'

Carers' Allowance

This taxable benefit is for informal carers including carers of children who have disabilities. You must be spending at least 35 hours a week caring for someone who is entitled to Disability Living Allowance. The amount received is not affected by savings you may have but is reduced if you earn over a certain amount a week. See www.directgov.uk.

Means tested Income Support

If your income is below a certain point and you are a carer/lone parent or unable to work then you may be eligible for Income Support. See www. directgov.uk.

The Family Fund

The Family Fund may be of relevance to families where the child has additional, severe problems. It is available to families on lower incomes or those entirely reliant on benefits and can give financial help with anything that is connected to the child's daily life and wellbeing, e.g. bedding, washing machines, family break holidays, hospital visiting costs and special play equipment. See www.familyfund.org.uk.

Special grants

It may be worth looking through grant directories in your local library or online to see if there are any grant-awarding organisations or charities that can help with particular costs involved in bringing up a child with special needs.

Direct payments

Many families of children with autism are eligible for direct payments from their local authority. This is where money for specific services or care is paid to the parent/carer for the child instead of the service being provided. This means the parent/carer can choose the appropriate help and support for their child themselves and have it covered financially.

Examples of direct payments being put to use include the following:

* Parents employ a helper/carer to look after the child who has autism so they can spend that time with their other children.

* Counselling or other needed therapy for a parent or carer.

* Respite care for the child.

Bear in mind that there are restrictions on what the payments can be used for. There will be reviews of the use and suitability of how you are using it and you may be required to contribute to some costs via means testing. The National Centre for Independent Living has further information and advice on its website, www.ncil.org.uk (see help list for details).

Carers UK has offices in England, Wales, Northern Ireland and Scotland and can give a great deal of advice and information on support for carers, www.carersuk.org (see help list for further details).

Home improvement

Grants or loans may be obtained from local authorities if you need to adapt your home for your child's needs. Each local authority has its own eligibility rules, so you will need to enquire.

Children Today Charitable Trust

This UK charity offers financial help towards the purchase of special equipment or sensory toys for children with special needs. Each applicant is assessed and means tested. See www.children-today.org.uk.

The Blue Badge scheme

Local authorities decide who is eligible for a Blue Badge. These entitle the holder to park in special bays or places that are nearer to their destination. Generally, the holder has a disability that makes walking a longer distance very difficult and may even mean the person cannot get to certain places at all. Children with autism may be physically able to walk but their anxiety and sensory issues may make certain areas or distances difficult, if not impossible, to cope with.

If this is the case with your child then you can apply for a Blue Badge. Your child's need may be assessed by an occupational therapist or other professional.

Read the two government leaflets *Can I get a Blue Badge?* (T/INF/1213) and *Blue Badges: Rights and Responsibilities* (T/INF/1214). You can find these online at www.dft.gov.uk/transportforyou/access/bluebadge by searching for the titles and reference numbers. Otherwise, contact the Blue Badge helpline – see help list for details.

'Blue Badge holders can park in special bays or places that are nearer to their destination.'

Continence Advisory Service

If your child is over the age of four and still incontinent, your local Continence Advisory Service may be able to discuss and organise free continence aids such as disposable pants and plastic sheeting. Ask your GP or health professional for more details.

Accessible toilets

Over 7,000 public toilets for the disabled in the UK are fitted with a special lock which can only be opened with a special key called a RADAR key. These keys are available to people with disabilities – you can apply for a key for your child online at www.radar.org.uk. The advantages in having such a key are that your child will not have to queue for the toilet and there is more room inside the cubicle for you as well if you need to go in to help.

Transport

If your child has a Statement of Special Educational Needs and has been allocated a place in a particular school (not necessarily a special needs school), you may be able to get help with transport or the cost of transport to and from school. Ask you local education authority about this.

If you do not have your own transport, some authorities have transport schemes for disabled or special needs children, e.g. the Ring-a-Ride minibus scheme in Oxfordshire. Contact your local authority or county council about similar schemes. If your area has such a scheme then your child's eligibility will be assessed.

Another scheme called Motability helps people with disabilities or their parents/carers to afford the cost of buying or hiring a car. You can only qualify for this if you are in receipt of the higher rate mobility component of the Disability Living Allowance. You can get further information from the Motability customer service helpline (see help list) or www.motability.co.uk.

'If your child has a Statement of Special Educational Needs and has been allocated a place in a particular school (not necessarily a special needs school), you may be able to get help with transport or the cost of transport to and from school.'

Summing Up

It is worth finding out if you and your family are entitled to any financial benefits. Bringing up a child who has autism is not easy and financial difficulties – even if only temporary – just add more pressure and stress to your lives. In addition to the allowances outlined in this chapter, it may also be worth finding out if there are other concessions or entitlements in your county or locality.

Chapter Nine

Getting Support

Mental health and family life

According to the National Autistic Society, parents of children with ASDs are almost twice as likely to experience emotional or psychological stress – 44% compared to 24% of parents with children without an ASD (National Autistic Society Appendix Three: Key Information About Autism).

Having a child with autism places a huge strain on parents and the whole family. The day-to-day caring and coping with your child's needs and behaviours can be emotionally and physically draining, and the stress can take its toll on your health and relationships. Although understanding, support and help does exist for families, there are many parents who, for one reason or another, still feel very much alone, unsupported and struggling. This may be for a number of reasons:

- They may have tried asking for help but not found the right resources.

- They may feel that others – friends, family, professionals – will judge their parenting skills if they admit they find it hard to cope.

- The services or help they need may not be offered or may be difficult to access where they live.

- They may not realise that their lives can feel different and better with support.

- They may believe that their needs are not great or deserving enough compared to the needs or struggles faced by many others.

To struggle on without support (ongoing if you need it) will only cause you more stress and may have a detrimental effect on all the family, your child with autism and your own mental health.

This chapter looks at some of the ways you can get help and support for yourself and your family.

Befriending schemes

Befriending schemes train volunteers to befriend a child (or adult) who has autism or their family. The befriender visits on a regular basis – perhaps once a week – and spends time with the child either at home or by taking them out to an enjoyable activity. While the benefits to the child are obvious, the parents and the rest of the family benefit from having a break from caring.

Contact the National Autistic Society's helpline to see if there are befriender and family support schemes in your area.

'Befriending schemes train volunteers to befriend a child (or adult) who has autism or their family.'

Family support schemes

Family support schemes – such as Autism Family Support in Oxfordshire – can also be a lifeline to parents and families who may feel they need a supportive and friendly source for information. Such schemes are especially helpful in the months following the diagnosis of a child as this can be a time when parents require a lot of advice. If you have such a project in your area, it may be able to put you in touch with support groups or other parents in similar situations.

In addition, you may have a local family centre or children's centre that could be a good place for you and your child to meet up with others. These sessions are normally for parents with very young or pre-school age children. Some have sessions for parents whose children have special needs. These centres may also be a good place to go if you need advice about health issues or local support.

The government initiated courses for carers may also be useful. These free programmes are usually run once a week for a number of weeks and suggest ways carers of children/adults who have a range of difficulties or disabilities can take care of their own needs. See www.direct.gov.uk – search for carers and learning.

National Autistic Society's Early Bird, Help and Help2 programmes

The National Autistic Society's Early Bird programme was set up to advise and support parents of pre-school age children who have recently been diagnosed with autism. The parents can attend group courses which teach strategies and helpful interventions to try with their child and they also receive home visits. The programme is not just a way of learning about useful interventions – it is a way of meeting other parents in the same situation and facing the same stresses and difficulties. Knowing you are not alone is very beneficial and some parents stay in touch with each other after the end of their programme. See www.autism.org/earlybird for more information.

Help and Help2 programmes are courses for parents of children on the autism spectrum and are held in regional locations throughout the UK. They are usually seminars and talks on issues such as managing behaviour and cover age ranges up to 18. These programmes have similar benefits as the Early Bird programmes. While they inform parents, they are also a source of advice and support, giving parents in similar situations the chance to meet and share views and ideas. Search for 'parent seminars' on the autism directory on the National Autistic Society's website (www.autism.org.uk/directory) or contact their autism helpline for more details. Nottingham Regional Society for Adults and Children with Autism, the Cambian Group and the Disabled Living Foundation also run seminars.

There is a small attendance charge for National Autistic Society courses. If this is too much, ask the National Autistic Society if there are sources of funding or where those eligible can get local funding for attending courses as a parent or carer.

'Knowing you are not alone is very beneficial and some parents stay in touch with each other after the end of their programme.'

Parent support groups – online or local

There are a number of online parent support groups which may be beneficial. Talking to other parents of children with autism or other conditions can help and you may be able to advise and support others as well as receiving understanding and support yourself. The Princess Royal Trust for Carers has an online discussion and chat forum.

Telephone support lines are another source of help. Parentline, Face to Face and the National Autistic Society helplines are examples. Another organisation called Carers UK has online information for carers that you might find useful. See help list for all contact details.

'Carers' centres can offer practical help, emotional support, training, breaks, befriending and advocacy.'

Contact a Family

This UK wide charity provides advice, information and support for parents of disabled children. What it offers parents includes:

▪ An online forum called www.makingcontact.org for parents to find and link up with others who have children/family members with the same medical problems or disorders.

▪ Local family support services.

▪ Guides and publications on a range of conditions and illnesses.

▪ Volunteer parent reps who offer local support and information.

You can contact this organisation by phone or email for advice and information if you feel you could benefit from their services. You can register online to join www.makingcontact.org.

Carers' centres

Carers' centres (set up by the Princess Royal Trust for Carers) are there for the parents and carers of children with autism too. Look at their website www.carers.org or ask your health professional for details of where to find your nearest one. Carers' centres can offer practical help, emotional support, training, breaks, befriending and advocacy. As well as centres, the charity's website has online discussion forums and chat rooms for carers to discuss their issues.

Counselling

Feeling you cannot cope with your situation or that you need emotional support to help you deal with particular issues might mean you would benefit from counselling. Counselling can be long term or short term. There are different types of counselling or therapy and you might want to investigate what type would be most beneficial to you. Some counsellors or therapists use more than one type.

Cognitive behavioural therapies

These include cognitive behaviour therapy (CBT), rational emotive behaviour therapy, solution focused therapy and acceptance and commitment therapy.

CBT is about helping people understand how their thoughts and behaviour impact upon their emotions. Clients are taught how to recognise irrational/negative thoughts and replace them with more accurate/pragmatic thoughts which help to bring about a change in perception, behaviour and emotion. CBT is recommended by NICE (the National Institute for Clinical Excellence) for the treatment of anxiety disorders and depression.

'CBT is about helping people understand how their thoughts and behaviour impacts upon their emotions.'

Psychodynamic

During psychodynamic therapy, the client learns how their experiences and personality influence their present thinking and situation. This therapy usually lasts longer than CBT.

Humanistic

Again, this therapy is more long term compared to CBT. The aim of the humanistic therapist is to believe in the client's capabilities and to allow them to move at their own pace. Types of humanistic therapy include the following:

- Person centred – the person's self concept is explored. The therapist listens empathetically and is non-judgemental, allowing the client to correct and develop their self-image.

- Gestalt – this is about promoting self awareness and the ability to support your own emotional needs.

- Transactional analysis – this is related to a theory that we have three 'ego states' which are 'parent', 'adult' and 'child' and that the way we are is the result of how we were treated and developed emotionally as children.

- Transpersonal psychology and psycho synthesis – here the client looks at their own personal view and is encouraged to discover deeper, spiritual aspects to themselves and so build on their qualities.

Mindfulness-based therapies

'Mindfulness meditation teaches you to stay in the present moment and see and accept your thoughts and feelings but not engage with them.'

Mindfulness-based therapies combine talking therapies with meditation. Mindfulness meditation teaches you to stay in the present moment and see and accept your thoughts and feelings but not engage with them. This method can help a person reduce stress and cope with ongoing difficult thoughts and situations. NICE recommends this type of therapy to help people avoid repeated bouts of depression. A good book to read about mindfulness is *The Mindful Way Through Depression* by Mark Williams and others.

The mental health charity MIND produces a booklet which explains the differences between the different types of therapy. The booklet is also downloadable from their website.

To find a counsellor, you could ask your GP to refer you or find a private therapist or counsellor by using the online search facility of one of the registering bodies for approved and registered therapists like the British

Association for Counselling and Psychotherapists (BACP) or the UK Council for Psychotherapy (UKCP). In addition, the National Autistic Society has a list of counsellors experienced in helping families affected by ASDs.

Having counselling can enable you to feel listened to and supported. It can make the difference between feeling overwhelmed with your anxieties and problems and finding a realistic way forward. Even those with close families and friendships can find the objective, empathetic and professional help that counsellors offer very beneficial.

Depression

Depression is an illness (not just a brief period of low mood) which can be triggered by stressful life events and having to cope with ongoing stress. Bringing up a child who has autism is an exhausting and stressful task which can take its toll on the mental health of parents. It is important to get professional medical advice and help if you are suffering from depression. Employing self-help techniques that work for you is good but you should also talk to your GP and get proper treatment if you have depression – even in its mildest form. A combination of talking therapy and medication is usually recommended. Medication should only ever be taken under the recommendation and ongoing supervision of your GP or medical professional.

'It is important to get professional medical advice and help if you are suffering from depression.'

Help in a crisis

If you ever feel overwhelmed by any pressures or stress and think that no one else is available to help, contact the Samaritans by phone or email. You don't have to be feeling suicidal to contact the Samaritans; they will listen and support anyone who contacts them in distress or with worries and concerns. Take a look at their website for advice as well: www.samaritans.org.

In addition, the charity Sane has a helpline for anyone in need of help and support because they are in mental distress (see help list).

Siblings

If you have other children, it is important to remember that having a sibling who has an ASD (or any other disability for that matter) can have a profound and lasting effect on children. Many siblings can develop insight and empathy into what it is like to live with a particular condition or disability and this is a positive and good thing. The knowledge and understanding they acquire can be beneficial later in life. However, it is important to remember that it can also be very difficult growing up with a brother or sister who has an ASD. The non-affected sibling may find that parents' attention is largely focused on the child with special needs and that they have to cope with their sibling's strange and difficult behaviours and the reactions of other people (which are not always positive). This can lead to the neuro-typical child resenting their brother or sister and the effect they have on you, the family and themselves.

'Try to enjoy some special time with your other children.'

- Teach your children that everyone is different, we all have different abilities and some people have particular difficulties. Be non-judgemental about this.

- While it is helpful to be flexible, do not allow autism to be an excuse for bad behaviour.

- Don't have double standards – treat all your children the same as far as possible.

- Encourage your other children's interests and their own friendships.

- Try to enjoy some special time with your other children.

- Don't expect your other children to be responsible for their brother or sister. It can be very common for siblings to worry about the future and who will care for the sibling who has autism (if they need caring for) once the parents are no longer alive.

- Let your neuro-typical children have space for themselves, e.g. their own room for their own possessions if possible.

- Encourage the caring attitude and insights your other children may develop as a result of having a sibling with a disability.

- Let your neuro-typical children talk to you about autism. They may wonder if they have it themselves or worry if their own children in the future will have ASDs. Don't let inaccurate and scary fears develop in your children's minds because you have not given them the chance to voice their concerns.

- Don't underestimate the impact on siblings. Very common reactions for siblings include anxiety, depression, over-attachments (being too dependent on someone) and delinquent behaviour.

- Check the National Autistic Society's website for books and helpful resources for siblings of children with autism.

- Check out Sibs, www.sibs.org.uk. This is the UK charity for siblings of brothers and sisters who have disabilities.

Your marriage/partnership

Research shows that having a child with autism can place a great strain on marriage and long term partnerships. The divorce rate for couples who have a child with autism is higher than the average. One American study claims it is around 80% (see 'Speaking Out On Autism', 31 October 2008, www.guardianweekly.co.uk). While no reliable statistics currently exist about autism and divorce in the UK, there is no doubt that most parents of children with autism are under a lot of stress (see 'Families: The Impact of Autism' on the National Autistic Society website). This article quotes some 1997 research that says 81.9% of parents sometimes felt 'stretched beyond their limit' and that a third of families never had a break or respite from the caring.

The strain that autism places on parents is due to many things and may include:

- The amount of effort needed to help the child – leaving the parents too exhausted and emotionally drained to give enough attention to other areas of their lives.

- Blaming one another for their child's difficulties.

- One parent taking the bulk of the responsibility for caring for the child with autism and resenting the partner who does less.

- Depression and anxiety.

However, if you have a partner there are many things you can do to help keep your marriage or partnership on track. Initially they may include:

- Finding out about autism and your child's condition together. Try to attend appointments together if possible.

- Sharing the care and parenting as much as possible.

- Allowing each other to react to your child's diagnosis in different ways. The National Autistic Society article 'Families: The Impact of Autism' also describes the different ways fathers and mothers often react – with mothers feeling that their child's diagnosis and ongoing care has the most negative impact on their lives.

- Explaining your child's autism and their needs to any close and trusted family members or friends, and accepting their help and support if offered.

- Making sure you have time away from your child just for yourselves and have that time regularly.

- Getting to know other parents who have children with ASDs.

- Finding and attending support groups/meetings for parents. Contact National Autistic Society helpline or your local services for information on any groups near you.

- Finding out about after school or out of school care schemes for children with special needs. These may be beneficial to your child and give you a break from the caring.

'Couple's counselling can be a good way of getting the support you both need at a difficult time.'

Couple's counselling

Couple's counselling can be a good way of getting the support you both need at a difficult time. It can enable you to talk through different issues, understand each other's point of view and find helpful ways forward.

Coping alone

If you are a single parent caring for a child with autism, you may feel that life is extra tough for you. For you, developing coping strategies and a good support system is even more vital. Getting a balance between caring for your child (and any other children if you have them) and getting your own needs met may feel like a real challenge at times. While you will have particular issues to deal with when managing your child's autism, you may find that the following resources offer useful advice, tips and support:

- www.loneparents.org – meet and chat to other lone parents online for tips and support.
- www.gingerbread.org.uk – factsheets, information and advice on a range of issues.
- *Single Parents – The Essential Guide* (Need2Know).

Taking a break – respite

When you have a child with autism, there will be times when you feel you need a break from caring. It is important to have time for yourself, for each other if you have a partner and for your family and other interests. Everyone needs the space to 'recharge their batteries' and to unwind from the inevitable stresses of bringing up a child who has special needs.

The kind of respite you need and may be entitled to will vary according to the severity of your child's autism or related disorders and your own individual situation.

Local autism support groups and organisations often organise holiday time activities for children on the spectrum to attend without their parents.

Some parents and families are able to organise their own informal 'respite' care with relatives or close friends who understand their child and are competent at caring for them. Your child may be able to spend a day (or even a few days) from time to time in someone else's care. If you are lucky enough to have such supportive help then use the time to enjoy the other relationships in your life or to give yourself the break you need.

'Everyone needs the space to "recharge their batteries" and to unwind from the inevitable stresses of bringing up a special needs child.'

Other parents use direct payments (see chapter 8) to employ a carer. Others can access respite facilities and resources in their area. Your local children's information services should be able to tell you what short break care and respite care is available and whether you are eligible. This can range from regular one or two night relief to longer occasional 'fostering'. This is where families with special needs children are linked up with other families willing and able to care for the child for a limited (perhaps regular) time. Families' individual circumstances are assessed to decide who is able to make use of these breaks.

In addition, you might also like the idea of specialist holiday locations/facilities designed for families with special needs children. These can cater for the whole family and often provide extra supervised times and activities each day for your child so that you can have a break. Many families who have children affected by autism find holidaying difficult, so these places that are understanding of you and your child's needs can be invaluable. Details of many of these can be found on the National Autistic Society's website.

'Many families who have children affected by autism find holidaying difficult, so places that are understanding of you and your child's needs can be invaluable.'

A life of your own

Difficult though it may be at times, make sure you have a life of your own. It can be easy to become so immersed in caring for your child and dealing with autism that you begin to give up aspects of your life that were once important and enjoyable to you. It is important not to give up the things that make you who you are.

Here are some useful tips to help you enjoy some time of your own:

- When you can, develop your job or career – even if only part-time.

- Keep in regular touch with friends.

- Do things you enjoy – developing hobbies and interests.

- Get emotional support through friendships and have more time with your partner if you have one.

- Meet other parents in the same situation.

- Join a support group for parents of children with ASDs or consider forming one if there isn't one near you.

Summing Up

The following are quotes from parents of children and teenagers on the spectrum. They sum up some of the things discussed in this chapter.

'Friends have been the best help – as well as trying to maintain a sense of humour.'

'I took up karate twice a week. I also saw a therapist just to talk things through and resolve my feelings.'

'Grandparents babysit for us about once or twice a year so that we can go away for a night or two and this is really helpful. I also think it is important to try and get some time doing something fun and relaxing even if it is just for an hour a week.'

'We … have the support of our Church and faith.'

'I really enjoy work and have supportive colleagues – we all talk about our various problems with our children.'

'I have recently had some counselling to help me come to terms with our family problems and I think it has helped.'

'Begin each day as a new start.'

'Support groups are excellent where many others have experienced the same issues.'

'Running is a good stress buster.'

'Keep in touch with friends and family.'

'Don't get lost in the autism. You are still you!'

'Keep laughing, find the good things that you enjoy doing and make the most of these.'

'As a parent, you want your child to reach their full potential – whatever that might be. You are your child's best ambassador. But when your child has autism, it can really take a lot out of you, so it's important to take care of yourself and get your own needs met too. Don't ever think you have to struggle when you can get help and support. When you do that, you are stronger – for yourself and for your child.'

Help List

AbilityNet

Tel: 0800 269545 (freephone)
enquiries@abilitynet.org.uk
www.abilitynet.org.uk
Advice and resources for those with disabilities who want to use adapted technology in the home or at work. Includes toys, IT equipment, software and voice output devices.

Ace Centre

92 Windmill Road, Oxford, OX3 7DR
Tel: 01865 759800
info@ace-centre.org.uk
www.ace-centre.org.uk
Includes advice and information on IT equipment for those with special needs.

Adviceguide

www.adviceguide.org.uk
The online Citizens Advice Bureau – provides information on rights, benefits, housing and employment. Also supplies information on debt, consumer and legal issues. Different sections are included for England, Scotland, Wales and Northern Ireland.

Advocacy for Education Service

Tel: 0845 070 4002
Advice and support over the phone for parents/carers of children with autism. Part of the National Autistic Society – see their website www.nas.org.uk.

After 16

www.after16.org.uk

A site for teenagers with special needs. Provides advice on finance, further education and work. Information for parents and professionals is also included.

Applied Behavioural Analysis (ABA)

See PEACH below or National Autistic Society website: shortcuts, A-Z (ABA).

The Association for Comprehensive Neurotherapy

PO Box 2198, Broken Arrow, OK 74013
acn@latitudes.org
www.latitudes.org
Complementary and alternative therapies for ADHD, Tourette's syndrome, autism and learning disabilities.

The Association of Dance Movement Therapy UK

ADMT UK, 32 Meadfoot Lane, Torquay, TQ1 2BW
admin@admt.org.uk
www.admt.org.uk
A register of qualified dance movement therapists.

Autism Management

www.autismmanagement.com
Links to information about autism including dietary interventions.

Autism Medical

www.autismmedical.com
Information about biomedical, allergy induced and autoimmune research.

Autism Research Centre (ARC)

Autism Research Centre, Section of Developmental Psychiatry, University of Cambridge, Douglas House, 18b Trumpington Road, Cambridge, CB2 8AH
Tel: 01223 746057
www.autismresearchcentre.com
Centre for research into autism. Useful and up-to-date information and links. Has the downloadable CHAT test.

Autism Research Institute

4182 Adams Avenue, San Diego, CA 92116, USA
www.autism.com
Concerned with conducting and fostering research in order to improve understanding of autism. Includes information on biomedical therapy.

Blue Badges

Tel: 02079442914 or 01613670009 (both helplines)
blue.badge@dft.gsi.gov.uk
www.dft.gov.uk/transportforyou/access/bluebadge
This is the link for the DfT booklet on who is eligible for a Blue Badge.

British Association of Art Therapists

24-27 White Lion Street, London, N1 9PD
Tel: 0207 686 4216
info@baat.org
www.baat.org
The professional organisation for art therapists in the UK, using art media as a primary mode of communication.

British Association for Counselling and Psychotherapists (BACP)

15 St John's Business Park, Lutterworth, Leicestershire, LE17 4HB
Tel: 01455 883316 (client information helpdesk)
01455 883300 (general inquiries)
www.bacp.co.uk
A professional registering body for counsellors. Has a find-a-therapist section. You can also call their client information line for help finding a suitable counsellor.

British Association of Dramatherapists

Waverley, Battledown Approach, Cheltenham, Gloucestershire, GL52 6RE
Tel: 01242 235515
enquiries@badth.org.uk
www.badth.org.uk

Professional body for dramatherapists in the UK. Uses healing aspects of drama and theatre as the therapeutic process. Help and advice about dramatherapy.

British Dyslexia Association

Unit 8, Bracknell Beeches, Old Bracknell Lane, Bracknell, RG12 7BW
Tel: 0845 2519002 (helpline)
helpline@bdadyslexia.org.uk
www.bdadyslexia.org.uk
Information about detecting dyslexia, advice and support.

Bullying UK

help@bullying.co.uk
www.bullying.co.uk
Help and advice for parents and pupils for dealing with school bullying.

Cambian Education Services Ltd

Tel: 0800 138 1184
www.cambianeducation.com
The largest provider of day and residential schools/colleges in England for children and young people affected by ASDs, including those with severe learning difficulties. Part of Cambian Group. Email form on website.

Carer's Allowance

www.directgov.org/en/CaringForSomeone/index.htm
Information on the allowance for those who look after someone with a disability.

Carers UK

20 Great Dover Street, London, SE1 4LX
Tel: 020 7378 4999
info@carers.uk.org
www.carersuk.org
Advice, support and information for carers.

CAT Kit

info@cat-kit.com
www.cat-kit.com
A method to teach and explore feelings, communication skills, behaviour and social skills for children with or without autism. Devised with the help of Tony Attwood, asperger/autism expert. Can be used by parents, teachers or counsellors and for small group or individual use. Email for details and cost of the kits.

The Challenging Behaviour Foundation

c/o The Old Courthouse, New Road Avenue, Chatham, Kent, ME4 6BE
Tel: 0845 602 7885 (family support line)
01634 838739 (general enquiries)
info@thecbf.org.uk
www.thecbf.org.uk
Information and support for parents, carers and professionals who look after children and adults with severe learning difficulties. Information sheets, DVDs, and details of local support networks.

Checklist for Autism in Toddlers (CHAT)

enquiries@paains.org.uk
www.paains.org.uk
The test developed to detect possible autism in toddlers. See the Public Autism Awareness website for information about the test, www.paains.org.uk.

Chewy Tubes

1 Sandbeck Way, Wetherby, West Yorkshire, LS22 7GH
Tel: 01937 580211
www.kapitex.com
This specialist company sells chewy tubes that are of use to children who like to bite or chew.

Children Today Charitable Trust

The Moorings, Rowton Bridge, Chestleton, Chester, CH3 7AE
Tel: 01244 335622
info@childrentoday.org.uk

www.children-today.org.uk
Provides grants for essential sensory equipment needed for children with
special needs.

Communication Matters

c/o The Ace Centre, 92 Windmill Road, Oxford, OX3 7DR
Tel: 0845 4568211
admin@communicationmatters.org.uk
www.communicationmatters.org.uk
Includes advice and information on IT equipment for those with special needs.

Confederation of Scottish Counselling Society (COSCA)

16 Melville Terrace, Stirling, FK8 2NE
Tel: 01786 475140
info@cosca.org.uk
www.cosca.org.uk
Professional body for counselling and psychotherapy in Scotland.

Contact a Family

209-211 City Road, London, EC1V 1JN
Tel: 0808 808 3555 (free helpline)
helpline@cafamily.org.uk
www.cafamily.org.uk
Provides information and support for parents of all disabled children. This is a
useful website for checking if you are getting the right benefits.

Council for Disabled Children

National Children's Bureau, 8 Wakley Street, London, EC1V 7QE
Tel: 020 7843 1900
cdc@ncb.org.uk
www.ncb.org.uk
The council works to influence national policy of issues that effect children with
disabilities. Has links to organisations that can provide help and support to
families.

Daily Life Therapy

See the Research Autism website.

DCSF Publications

England:

Sanctuary Buildings, Great Smith Street, London, SW1P 3BT
Tel: 0870 000 2288 (9am-5pm, Monday to Friday)
info@dcsf.gsi.gov.uk
www.dcsf.gov.uk

Wales:

Welsh Assembly Government, Cathays Park, Cardiff, CF10 3NQ
Tel: 0845 010 3300
webmaster@wales.gsi.gov.uk
www.wales.gov.uk

Scotland:

Scottish Government, Victoria Quay, Edinburgh, EH6 6QQ
Tel: 08457 741 741
ceu@scotland.gsi.gov.uk
www.scotland.gov.uk

Northern Ireland (Department of Education):

Rathgael House, Balloo Road, Bangor, BT19 7PR
Tel: 028 9127 9279
mail@deni.go.uk
www.deni.gov.uk

See website and publications for information about education and special needs provision.

Delacato Clinic

The Autism Centre, 26 Gwscwm Park, Burry Port, Llanelli, Carmarthenshire, SA16 ODX
Tel: 01554 836960
www.theautismcentre.co.uk

Devises therapy programmes for children with neurological disorders. Assesses children and teaches parents how to implement the programme at home.

Department for Work and Pensions

www.dwp.gov.uk
Information about benefits and how to claim them.

Disability Alliance UK

Universal House, 88-94 Wentworth Street, London, E1 7SA
Tel: 020 7247 8776
office.da@dial.pipex.com
www.disabilityalliance.org
Provides information and advice on issues faced by disabled people. The
telephone number is not an advice line.

Disability Discrimination Act

www.direct.gov.uk/en/DisabledPeople/RightsAndObligations/DisabilityRights
Includes information for employers and employees on workplace regulations
and support for disabled people in the workplace.

Disability Living Allowance

www.directgov.org
Click on the link 'disabled people'. Information on the tax free benefit for those
who need personal care or help with walking.

Disabled Living Foundation

380-384 Harrow Road, London, W9 2HU
Tel: 0845 130 9177 (helpline, 10am-4pm, Monday to Friday)
info@dlf.org.uk
www.dlf.org.uk
Free advice on independent living solutions, e.g. where to get particular
products or find suppliers of useful items for those with disabilities.

Disabled Students Allowance

www.directgov.uk
Help for English students with disabilities who need extra finance due to their
disability to undertake further or higher education or Open University courses.

Driver and Vehicle Licensing Agency (DVLA)

www.dvla.gov.uk
See their website for information on Blue Badges.

The Dyspraxia Foundation

8 West Alley, Hitchin, Herts, SG5 1EG.
Tel: 01462 454 986 (helpline, 10am-1pm, Monday to Friday)
dyspraxia@dyspraxiafoundation.org.uk
www.dyspraxiafoundation.org.uk
Information, support and advice for those affected by or dealing with others affected by dyspraxia.

Education and Resources for Improving Childhood Continence (ERIC)

36 Old School House, Britannia Road, Kingswood, Bristol, BS15 8DB
Tel: 0845 370 8008 (helpline, 10am-4pm, Monday to Friday)
info@eric.org.uk
www.eric.org.uk
The UK charity giving advice, information and helpline support to parents and carers of incontinent children.

Face2Face

Tel: 0844 800 9189
face2facenetwork@scope.org.uk
www.face2facenetwork.org.uk
Nationwide and online support and befriending service for parents of disabled children.

The Family Fund

4 Alpha Court, Monks Cross Drive, York, YO32 9WN
Tel: 0845 130 4542 or 01904 621115
info@familyfund.org.uk
www.familyfund.org.uk
Organisation that gives grants to eligible families of children with severe disabilities.

Family Safe Plus+

Community Alerts Ltd, Bridge House, Bridge Road Business Park, Haywards Heath, West Sussex, RH16 1TX
Tel: 0870 062 4919
info@familysafeplus.co.uk
www.familysafeplus.co.uk
Safety tags for your child to wear with emergency contact details. You can also register your family's details with the company and these can be accessed and used in an emergency.

Fledglings

Wenden Court, Station Approach, Wenders Ambo, Saffron Walden, Essex, CB11 4LB
Tel: 0845 458 1124 (helpline)
enquiries@fledglings.org.uk
www.fledglings.org.uk
Free product searches for families with special needs children. Can supply or suggest supplier.

Fragile X Society

Rood End House, 6 Stortford Road, Great Dunmow, Essex, CM6 1DA
Tel: 01371 875100
info@fragilex.org.uk
www.fragilex.org.uk
Information, support, research details for those with fragile X syndrome and their families.

Gingerbread

255 Kentish Town Road, London, NW5 2LX
Tel: 0800 018 5026 (single parent helpline)
020 7428 5400 (general enquiries)
info@gingerbread.org.uk for general enquiries
www.gingerbread.org.uk
A support organisation for single parents. Has other regional offices.

Hanen

www.hanen.org
Gives an overview of the Hanen approach. Hanen is a Canadian organisation but therapists in the UK can attend training programmes here. See also I CAN.

Hendrickx Associates

11 Connaught Road, Hove, East Sussex, BN3 3WB
Tel: 01273 711258
info@asperger-training.com
www.asperger-training.com
Training, counselling, assessments and advice for organisations and individuals affected by ASDs and other types of neuro-diversity.

Horizon School for Children with Autism

Blithbury Road, Blithbury, Rugeley, Staffordshire, WS15 3JQ
Tel: 01889 504400
horizonschool@priorygroup.com
A residential special school.

I CAN

8 Wakley Street, London, EC1V 7QE
Tel: 0845 225 4071
www.ican.org.uk
I CAN is a charity working to support the development of speech, language and communication skills in all children with a special focus on those with special needs in this field. Advice and resources for parents. Runs workshops and training days for teachers and therapists including the Hanen method programme.

Income Support

See www.directgov.org and look under the 'money, tax and benefits' link.

Irlen

Irlen East, 4 Park Farm Business Centre, Fornham, Saint Genevieve, Bury St Edmunds, Suffolk, IP28 6TS

Tel: 01284 724301
info@irleneast.com
www.irleneast.com
Information about light sensitivity in connection with other conditions. Suppliers of colour filter glasses that help deal with visual sensory disturbances.

Lego® therapy

See Autism Research Centre, Cambridge. Click on the 'news and events' link for articles on lego therapy. Also see National Autistic Society website.

Listening Programme®

Learning Solutions, The Villa, 1 Hollingwood Lane, Bradford, West Yorkshire, BD7 2RE
Tel: 01274 777250 (9.30am-5pm)
info@learning-solutions.co.uk
www.learning-solutions.co.uk
A music-based auditory stimulation method of helping children with autism.

Lone Parents

www.lone-parents.org.uk
A virtual meeting place for single parents to find advice and support. Chat room and forum available. Use the online enquiry form to contact them.

Lorna Wing Centre for Autism (The National Autistic Society)

Elliot House, 113 Masons Hill, Bromley, Kent, BR2 9HT
Tel: 020 8466 0098
elliot.house@nas.org.uk
www.autism.org.uk
Any enquiries regarding diagnosis should be directed to the National Autistic Society helpline on 0845 070 4004 and not to the centre itself.
A diagnostic, assessment and advice centre for children and adults with ASDs. The website has information on how to get a referral and how a diagnosis may be made.

Makaton

The Makaton Charity, Manor House, 46 London Road, Blackwater, Camberley, Surrey, GU17 0AA
Tel: 01276 606760
info@makaton.org
www.makaton.org
A structured language programme that uses signs and symbols.

MIND

15-19 Broadway, London, E15 4BQ
Tel: 0845 766 0163 (info line, 9am-5pm, Monday to Friday)
contact@mind.org.uk
MIND Cymru
3rd Floor, Quebec House, Castlebridge, 5-19 Cowbridge Road East, Cardiff, CF11 9AB
Tel: 029 2039 5123
www.mind.org.uk
Local support and advice groups for those affected by poor mental health. Website provides useful advice and information, details of publications and a 'find your nearest' group directory.

Motability

Motability Operations, City Gate House, 22 Southwark Bridge Road, London, SE1 9HB
Tel: 0845 456 4566
www.motability.co.uk
The motability scheme enables disabled people to use their motability allowance to buy a car, powered wheelchair or scooter. Use online enquiry form to contact them.

National Autistic Society

England and Head Office:
393 City Road, London, EC1V 1NG
Tel: 0845 070 4004 (helpline)
nas@nas.org.uk

Cymru:
6-7 Village Way, Greenmeadow Springs Business Park, Tongwynlais, Cardiff, CF15 7NE
Tel: 02920 629 312
wales@nas.org.uk

Scotland:
Central Chambers, 1st Floor, 109 Hope Street, Glasgow, G2 6LL
Tel: 0141 221 8090
scotland@nas.org.uk

Northern Ireland:
57A Botanic Avenue, Belfast, BT7 1JL
Tel: 02890 236 235
northern.ireland@nas.org.uk
www.autism.org.uk

Leading UK charity with branches in Scotland, Northern Ireland, Wales and England. Promotes awareness and knowledge of ASDs. This charity's vast and in-depth website gives details of just about every issue that affects the person with ASD and their family as well as professionals, employers and teachers. Their Prospects programme helps young people with autism to train and find work. Their Help and Help2 team produce a resource sheet with information about sources for obtaining visual supports, communication aids, personal care items, safety devices, etc. Also follow their website links for information on creating autism friendly environments and details of suppliers of safety products and robust play equipment. Also produced 'Families: The Impact of Autism'.

National Centre for Independent Living

Unit 3.40, Canterbury Court, 1-3 Brixton Road, London, SW9 6DE
Tel: 0207 587 1663
info@ncil.org.uk
www.ncil.org.uk

A resource for independent living. Directory of local support services has information on direct payments.

National Institute for Health and Clinical Excellence (NICE)

London:
MidCity Place, 71 High Holborn, London, WC1V 6NA
Tel: 0845 003 7780
nice@nice.org.uk
Manchester:
Level 1A, City Tower, Piccadilly Plaza, Manchester, M1 4BD
Tel: 0845 003 7780
nice@nice.org.uk
www.nice.org.uk
An independent organisation providing national guidance on health issues.

The National Light and Sound Therapy Centre

80 Queen Elizabeth's Walk, London, N16 5UQ
Tel: 0208 880 1269
zl@light-and-sound.co.uk
www.light-and-sound.co.uk
NHS provider offering specialised treatment for a variety of disabilities
including autism. Has pioneered AIT Plus programme which aims to make a
difference to some of the most distressing symptoms.

Natobe Safety

Portsmouth Technopole, Kingston Crescent, Portsmouth, PO2 8FA
Tel: 023 9271 2293
www.natobe.co.uk
Sells wander alarms to attach to your child which will alert you if they stray too
far.

Nottingham Regional Society for Adults and Children with Autism

Park Hall Autism Resource Centre, Park Road, Bestwood Village, Nottingham,
NG6 8TQ
Tel: 0115 976 1805
norsacaadmin@btconnect.com
www.norsaca.org.uk

Charity that supports adults and children with autism in the Nottinghamshire and Derbyshire area. Advice, counselling, parent workshops, day and residential schools for those with ASDs.

Oaasis

The Croft, Vicars Hill, Boldre, Lymington, Hants, SO41 5QB
Tel: 0800 197 3907 (helpline)
oassis@cambiangroup.com
www.oaasis.co.uk
Website giving information for those caring for children with autism, Asperger's and other learning difficulties.

OCD Action

Suites 506-509, Davina House, 137-149 Goswell Road, London, EC1V 7ET
Tel: 0845 390 6232/020 7253 2664 (support and information)
support@ocdaction.org.uk
www.ocdaction.org.uk
Help, information and support groups for those with OCD.

The Office of the Public Guardian

PO Box 15118, Birmingham, B16 6GX
Tel: 0845 330 2900 (9am-5pm, Monday, Tuesday, Thursday and Friday, 10am-5pm, Wednesdays)
customerservices@publicguardian.gsi.gov.uk
www.publicguardian.gov.uk
Home Office department that advises on legal matters regarding the care and financial issues of those unable to take care of themselves in these respects. Information on how to make arrangements and booklets, forms and applications.

Oxford Autism Research Group

University Department of Psychiatry, Warneford Hospital, Oxford, OX3 7JX
Tel: 01865 226515
autism.research@psych.ox.ac.uk
www.psychiatry.ox.ac.uk/autism

Current research and information about autism and Asperger's syndrome, including information on the MEG scanner. Website includes useful links for professionals and families.

Parentline

Parentline Plus
520 Highgate Studios, 53-79 Highgate Road, Kentish Town, London, NW5 1TL
Tel: 0808 800 2222 (helpline)
www.parentlineplus.org.uk

Parentline Scotland
Tel: 0808 800 2222
www.children1st.org.uk
Advice and guidance for parents via telephone support or email.

Peach

The Brackens, London Road, Ascot, Berkshire, SL5 8BE
Tel: 01344 882248
www.peach.org.uk
A parent led group, Peach supports and informs parents of children with autism. Peach is the fastest growing UK charity in the field of Applied Behavioural Analysis (ABA) and autism.

Pet therapy
See Research Autism website.

The Picture Exchange Communication System (PECS)

Pyramid Educational Consultants UK, Pavillion House, 6 Old Steine, Brighton, BN1 1EJ
Tel: 01273 609555
pyramid@pecs.org.uk
www.pecs.org.uk
Providers of training, consultation and support to parents, carers and professionals involved with children and adults with communication difficulties.

Play and Language for Autistic Youngsters (PLAY)

1601 Briarwood Circle, Suite 500, Ann Arbor, MI 48108
info@playproject.org
www.playproject.org
Details and information on PLAY, a community based autism training and early intervention programme.

The Princess Royal Trust for Carers

Unit 14, Bourne Court, Southend Road, Woodford Green, Essex, IG8 8HD
Tel: 0844 800 4361
info@carers.org
www.carers.org
Advice, support and discussion forums for carers.

RADAR – The Disability Network

12 City Forum, 250 City Road, London, EC1V 8AF
Tel: 0207 2503222
radar@radar.org.uk
www.radar.org.uk
A disability campaigning organisation. Keys for public disabled toilets can be applied for from this organisation.

Raising Horizons

16 Brough Road, South Cave, Brough, HU15 2BX

Tel: 01482 651695
info@raisinghorizons.com
www.raisinghorizons.com
An organisation that seeks to develop and offer training materials to those with autism and other learning difficulties.

Reflexology International

Ann Gillanders, Reflexology International, 92 Sheering Road, Old Harlow, Essex, CM17 0JW
Tel: 01279 429060
www.footreflexology.com

Information about reflexology including directory of practitioners.

Research Autism

Church House, Church Road, Filton, Bristol, BS34 7BD
Tel: 020 8292 8900
info@researchautism.net
www.researchautism.net
The UK charity that carries out research into the different interventions in autism.

Rett Syndrome Association UK

Langham House West, Mill Street, Luton, LU1 2NA
Tel: 01582 798910
info@rettsyndrome.org.uk
www.rettsyndrome.org.uk
A national charity for people living with Rett syndrome. Information, advice, research, campaigns, etc.

The Royal College of Speech and Language Therapists

2 White Hart Yard, London, SE1 1NX
Tel: 020 7378 1200
www.rcslt.org
The professional body for speech and language therapists and support workers.

Samaritans

Chris, PO Box 9090, Stirling, FK8 2SA
Tel: 08457 909090 (UK)
1850 609090 (Republic of Ireland)
www.samaritans.org
24-hour telephone helpline offering emotional support for people who are experiencing feelings of distress or despair, including those that may lead to suicide.

SANE

1st Floor Cityside House, 40 Adler Street, London, E1 1EE
Tel: 0845 767 8000 (helpline, 6pm-11pm)
sanemail@sane.org.uk
www.sane.org.uk
SANEline and SANEmail offer emotional support and information to those experiencing mental health problems, their families and carers.

Sensory Direct

Tel: 0800 0837212
www.sensory-direct.co.uk
Special weighted items that help those with sensory issues, including weighted blankets and lap pads. Email form on website.

Sensory Processing Disorder Resource Center

www.sensory-processing-disorder.com
An online resource centre for purchasing items and equipment that help deal with a variety of sensory issues. Also information on how to devise an autism friendly environment/room. Email form on website.

Sibs

Meadowfield, Oxenhope, West Yorkshire, BD22 9JD
Tel: 01535 645453
www.sibs.org.uk
Support organisation for child and adult siblings of children with special needs. Email form on website.

Social Stories™

The Gray Center for Social Learning and Understanding, c/o City on a Hill Ministries, 100 Pine Street, Suite 121, Zeeland, MI 49464
info@thegraycenter.org
www.thegraycenter.org
or
1508 N.E. 130th. St. Vancouver, Washington 98685
info@socialstories.com

www.socialstories.com
Invented by Carol Gray in the 1990s. Stories to help the learning and development of those with ASDs.

Son-Rise

www.autismtreatmentcenter.org
A US based organisation, the Autism Treatment Center of America provides treatment/intervention programmes for adults and children affected by autism. They sometimes run training courses for parents in the UK too. Email form on website.

Sparklebox

enquiries@sparklebox.co.uk
www.sparklebox.co.uk
A website for teachers/parents that provides free printable signs, letters, pictures, etc for young children.

Special Needs Pushchairs

Chariots All Terrain Pushchairs, Orchard Farm, Spreyton, Nr Crediton, Devon, EX17 5AS
Tel: 01363 881 110
sales@specialneedspushchairs.co.uk
www.specialneedspushchairs.co.uk
Larger and stronger pushchairs for older children with special needs.

TEACCH

www.teacch.com
Treatment and education of autistic and related communication-handicapped children. See website for details of regional centres.

TFH Special Needs

5-7 Severnside Business Park, Severn Road, Stourport on Severn, Worcestershire, DY13 9HT
Tel: 01299 827 820
info@tfhuk.com

www.specialneedstoys.com
Age appropriate toys for those with special needs.

Therapy Shoppe

PO Box 8875, Grand Rapids, MI 49518
thershoppe@aol.com
www.therapyshoppe.com
Therapy merchandise and speciality toys and gadgets.

Tony Attwood

www.tonyattwood.com.au
Informative website of clinical psychologist, author and leading Asperger's
syndrome expert. Has links to recent research reports.

Tough Furniture Ltd

Stokewood Road, Craven Arms Business Park, Craven Arms, Shropshire, SY7
8NR
Tel: 01588 674 340
sales@toughfurniture.com
www.toughfurniture.com
Sturdy furniture that can withstand rough treatment.

Transporters

Changing Media Development Ltd, 2 Sheraton Street, London, W1F 8BH
www.thetransporters.com
Here you can order a special DVD of *Thomas the Tank Engine and Friends*
that enhances the development of the understanding of emotion and facial
expression in ASD children.

UK Council for Psychotherapy (UKCP)

2nd Floor Edward House, 2 Wakley Street, London, EC1V 7LT
Tel: 020 7014 9955
info@ukcp.org.uk
www.psychotherapy.org.uk
Register of qualified and registered counsellors/therapists.

Book List

1001 Great Ideas for Teaching and Raising Children with Autism Spectrum Disorders
By Ellen Notbohm and Veronica Zysk, Future Horizons, USA, 2005.

Adolescents on the Autism Spectrum
By Chantal Sicile-Kira, Perigree, Vermilion, London, 2007.

Animals in Translation: Using the Mysteries of Autism to Decode Animal Behaviour
By Temple Grandin and Catherine Johnson, Scribner, USA, 2004.

Aromatherapy and Massage for People with Learning Difficulties
By Helen Sanderson, Jane Harrison and Shirley Price, Hands on Publishing, USA, 1991.

Autism, Play and Social Interaction
By Lone Gammeltoft and Marianne Sollock Nordenhof, Jessica Kingsley Publishers, London, 2007

Autism: The Search for Coherence
By Sheila Coates and John Richer, Jessica Kingsley Publishers, London, 2001.

The Autistic Spectrum
By Lorna Wing, Constable and Robinson, London, 1996.

Boys Guide to Becoming a Teen
By the American Medical Association and Kate Gruenwald Pfeifer, Jossey Bass, USA, 2006.

Caring for Myself
By Christy Gast and Jane Krug, Jessica Kingsley Publishers, London, 2008.

Challenging Behaviour and Autism: Making Sense, Making Progress
By Philip Whitaker, Helen Joy, Jane Harley and David Edwards, National Autistic Society, London, 2001.

Creating an Autism Friendly Environment
By A Nguyen, National Autistic Society, London, 2006.

Daily Life Therapy: A Method of Educating Autistic Children
By K Kitahara, Nimrod Press, USA, 1984.

Everybody is Different: A Book for Young People Who Have Brothers or Sisters with Autism
By Fiona Bleach, National Autistic Society, London, 2001.

Girls Growing Up on the Autism Spectrum: What Parents and Professionals Should Know about the Pre-teen and Teenage Years
By Shana Nichols, Jessica Kingsley Publishers, London, 2008.

A Guide to the Mental Capacity Act 2005
By J Butcher, National Autistic Society, London, 2007.

Home Educating Our Autistic Spectrum Children: Paths Are Made By Walking
By Terri Dowty, Jessica Kingsley Publishers, London, 2001.

I Have Autism…What's That?
By Kate Doherty, Paddy McNally and Eileen Sherrard, Down Lisburn Trust, Belfast, 2000.

The Incredible 5-point Scale: Assisting Children with Autism Spectrum Disorders in Understanding Social Interactions and Controlling Their Emotional Responses
By Kari Dunn Buron and Mitzi Curtis, Autism Asperger Publishing Co, USA, 2003.

Making Sense of Counselling
By Jocelyn Catty, MIND, London, 2004.

The Mindful Way Through Depression: Freeing Yourself from Chronic Unhappiness
By Mark Williams, John Teasdale, Zindel Segal and Jon Kabat-Zinn, Guildford Press, USA, 2007.

My Child Won't Sleep: Practical Advice and Guidance on the Common Sleeping Problems of Young Children
By J Douglas and N Richman, Penguin Books, London, 1988.

My Family is Different: A Workbook for Children with a Brother or Sister Who has Autism or Asperger Syndrome
By Carolyn Brock, National Autistic Society, London, 2007.

Revealing the Hidden Social Code: Social Stories™ for People with Autistic Spectrum Disorders
By Marie Howley and Eileen Arnold, Jessica Kingsley Publishers, London, 2003.

Sleep Better! A Guide to Improving Sleep for Children with Special Needs
By V Mark Durand, Brookes Publishing Co, USA, 1997.

Taking Care of Myself: A Hygiene, Puberty and Personal Curriculum for Young People with Autism
By Mary Wrobel, Future Horizons, USA, 2003.

Talking Together About Growing Up: A Workbook for Parents of Children with Disabilities
By Lorna Scott and Lesley-Kerr Edwards, The Family Planning Association, London, 1999

Talking Together About Sex and Relationships: A Practical Resource for Schools and Parents Working with Young People with Learning Disabilities
By Lorna Scott and Lesley Kerr-Edwards, The Family Planning Association, London, 2003.

When My Autism Gets Too Big: A Relaxation Book for Children with Autism Spectrum Disorders
By Kari Dunn Buron, Autism Asperger Publishing, USA, 2004.

Yoga for Children with Autistic Spectrum Disorder
By D and S Betts, Jessica Kingsley Publishers, London, 2006.

Your Child and You: A Guide for Parents and Carers of Disabled Children and Children with Additional Needs
By Oxfordshire Children's Information Service, Witney, 2004.

Glossary

Attention deficit (hyperactivity) disorder (ADD/ADHD)
A biological condition that results in impulsive and inattentive behaviour. Some with the condition are also hyperactive.

Autoimmune
It is called an autoimmune disease when a person's immune system attacks itself. Examples are diabetes, rheumatoid arthritis and multiple sclerosis.

Asperger's syndrome
A form of high functioning autism. Those with Asperger's syndrome have the same kind of difficulties that those with autism have but are less severely affected. It is possible to go through life without ever having the diagnosis.

Biochemical/biomedical
Biochemical means the study of the chemical composition or processes that go on in our bodies, such as how wo are affected by proteins, etc. Biomedical is the study of how our bodies process nutrients, or whatever they are exposed to, and the way various toxins, diets, etc affect our mental and physical health.

CHAT
A developmental test for toddlers administered by GPs or other health professionals. The result indicates whether or not the child has signs of having an ASD.

Co-morbid condition
A condition a person suffers from alongside, or in addition to, the main one, e.g. someone who has an ASD might also have dyslexia.

Dyslexia
A learning difficulty mainly connected with reading, writing and spelling.

Dyspraxia
A motor or movement co-ordination disability.

Echolalia
The habit of, or need to, repeat a sound or words just heard, usually out loud.

Fragile X syndrome
An inherited mental impairment condition similar to autism. See
www.fragilex.org.uk for more information.

Genetics
The study of hereditary conditions or features and how these are passed from
parents to their children.

High functioning autism
Someone who has a diagnosis of autism at the higher end of the autism
spectrum. They have fewer difficulties and in many areas are considered
intelligent or even highly intelligent.

Kanner's syndrome
A more severe form of autism in which language develops later or not at all.

Neurology/neurological
Refers to the way the brain and nervous system works. A neurological disorder
is one that is caused by the brain or nervous system working in a way that is
not normal.

Neuro-typical
A person whose brain patterns/behaviours are considered normal.

OCD
An anxiety disorder in which people affected have constant unwelcome,
intrusive thoughts and perform behaviours to relieve themselves of the anxiety
these thoughts evoke.

Pervasive developmental disorder not otherwise specified (PDD-NOS)
The term refers to those people who have difficulties in more than one area but
do not fulfil the diagnostic criteria for autism or Asperger's syndrome.

Proprioceptors
Internal sensory organs found in muscles, joints and tendons which detect
movements and position of the body.

Prosody
The rhythm of speech.

Rett syndrome

An autism related condition. A person with Rett syndrome may have identifiable physical differences such as reduced muscle tone or floppiness. There is also a chromosomal difference. It affects mainly girls. See www.rettsyndrome.org.uk for more information.

Ritualistic behaviour

This can be always wanting to do something a certain way or insisting that things are always a certain way.

Stimming

A self-stimulatory, repetitive action that comforts the person performing it. Stimming can include repetitive vocal sounds, hand flapping, tapping feet or finger flicking.

Tourette's syndrome

A neurological disorder that causes uncontrollable tics. They may be physical (e.g. jerking the head or throwing an arm up in the air) or verbal (e.g. shouting out a particular word, maybe swearing).

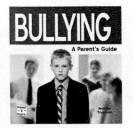